DATE DUE

MR 7 '97			
MR 21 '97			
MY 22 00			
NO 28 04			

DEMCO 38-296

CALIFORNIA WOMEN SPEAK

Speeches of California Women in Public Office

Introduction by Kate Karpilow

Doris Earnshaw, Editor

Published by

Alta Vista Publishing Company
P.O. Box 73675
Davis, California 95617

Cover Photograph by Ian Martin

Photographs of Joyce Kennard, Anne Rudin, and Sandra Smoley
by Sirlin Photographers, Sacramento, California

The speeches in the book are printed by permission.

ISBN: 0-9640574-0-9

Printed in the United States of America

Dedicated to All California Women

in Public Service

Acknowledgments:

My thanks first to Assemblywoman Delaine Eastin for her rousing speech at the University of California, Davis, included here, which rekindled my long-felt desire to publish speeches of women in public office. My thanks also to Ann M. Evans and Kate Karpilow who have guided, advised and inspired me; Terry Antonelli, the first reader; Patricia Bulman, Muriel Feinstein, Cairn Rominger, David Thompson, Patti Vernelson, Jeanne Pietrzak and special thanks to Mary Doty.

Table of Contents

Preface

Although women have long felt the impact of public policy, they have long been barred from its creation. Until recently, women rarely spoke in public, could not vote, could not hold elected office. They had no public voice.

Two decades ago, Dr. Doris Earnshaw began her quest for women's voices by gathering women's poetry written worldwide. She brought the voice of these poets to life in the anthology, *The Other Voice: Twentieth Century Women Poets in Translation*. Just as women's artistic works are not as well-known as men's, women's political work is not known. If you want to quote from the words of an elected woman, there are no sources. Despite a record number of women seeking and winning elected office since 1980, the political voice of women is virtually unpublished, unheard.

In her new work, *California Women Speak*, Dr. Earnshaw brings together the firsthand accounts of why California-elected women run for office, what problems they want to solve, and how they intend to deal with the critical issues facing California and the nation.

These speeches illustrate that elected women bring a needed, new approach to California politics. They live in a state teeming with problems that people in other states just read about, with a budget deficit larger than most states' budgets. These women, many of whom first gained experience in local organizations and local government, address the everyday needs of people—health, jobs and housing. They stress cooperative solutions, and they protect the public purse as they do the family budget.

Elected women are using the public forum to counter the historic advantage of elected men whose normal ascent to power includes access to all-male inner circles on the golf course, in private clubs, and, until recently, in the halls of legislatures and businesses across the land. Women are reaching out to the public to create momentum for their ideas. They are dispelling the myths about women and power: that women do not know the issues, that women do not "look the part" of elected officials, that women cannot inspire leadership through force of presence. Public speaking, therefore, serves additional purposes in the world of elected women. *California Women Speak* illuminates the world they believe is worth fighting for.

Elected women have found their public voice. This book allows their eloquence to be heard.

Ann M. Evans
Chief of Staff, Assemblywoman Delaine Eastin
Mayor, City of Davis (1984-1986)

Introduction

1992 was lauded by many as the "year of the political woman;" and in California, it was in some ways a year to celebrate.

1992 was the first time ever that California voters elected a woman to serve in the United States Senate. In a typically California spirit, we not only elected one woman, but two, thus becoming the first state in the nation to elect two women, Dianne Feinstein and Barbara Boxer, to serve simultaneously as our representatives in the United States Senate.

An historic increase also took place in California's elections for the House of Representatives, where the number of women serving in California's Congressional delegation doubled, increasing from three women out of 45 (7 percent) to seven women out of a total of 52 (13 percent). The increase in the total number of seats was due to redistricting.

While many factors came together in 1992 to bring about wins for elected women, many observers of women in politics add a sobering context for these successes. In February, 1994, (as this book goes to press), women still comprise only 7 percent of the members in the United States Senate and 11 percent in the House of Representatives. In California, women comprise only 13 percent of the state Senate, 29 percent of the state Assembly, and hold less than a third of the city council and board of supervisors seats throughout the state.

Parity is still decades away.

Moreover, despite steady political gains for women in the last 20 years and the victories of 1992, there is little or no permanent record of their speeches, no means to pass on the words, ideas, and visions that have persuaded citizens to vote for women and encouraged colleagues to support their legislation.

The purpose of *California Women Speak* is to give voice to the women who are serving or who have served in elected office in the state of California and to inspire the women who will follow in their footsteps.

Why California? Long recognized as a trend-setter in areas as diverse as music, computer technology and the media, 1992 proved that California was once again on the cutting edge in government and politics. Moreover, the state's population is the largest and most diverse in the country; and the voting patterns of our electorate, the issues that our elected officials must respond to and the complexity of governing this jurisdiction of 30-plus million people in many ways portend the future of many states, if not the nation itself.

In *California Women Speak,* you will hear from Democrats and Republicans and a strong-willed Independent, seasoned incumbents and newcomers, passionate orators and more deliberate communicators. The women serve at many levels of office—from the United States Senate to city councils, from constitutional offices to the state Legislature, from the California

Supreme Court to the Sacramento Municipal Court. Many of the women have served in more than one office, reflecting their commitment to public service.

The 16 women profiled in *California Women Speak* are political pioneers. Almost every woman who speaks out in the following pages can point to at least one "first" in her background. Dianne Feinstein was the first woman candidate from a major party to run for governor of the state. Joyce Kennard was the first woman of color to be appointed to the California State Supreme Court, and only the second woman to serve in the court's history. Sandra Smoley was the first woman elected to the Sacramento County Board of Supervisors.

These pioneers have gone to great lengths to learn their craft, not only becoming experts in traditional women's issues, such as health, education and welfare, but also breaking stereotypes and becoming experts in foreign policy, the economy and the environment.

Congresswoman Nancy Pelosi, as chair of the Congressional Working Group on China, speaks both eloquently and persuasively on the need to condition most-favored-nation status for China on improvements in human rights. Former Sacramento Mayor Anne Rudin argues that the state's capital should implement a peace-promoting foreign policy. State Senator Marian Bergeson displays a firm grasp of government finance with a savvy analysis of the abuses of redevelopment financing. In a speech to the Planning and Conservation League, then-Congresswoman Barbara Boxer, now United States senator, demonstrates a commanding knowledge of the state's environmental and natural resource issues.

Many of the women go beyond simply addressing the issues to add a very personal dimension to their remarks. Not only does state Treasurer Kathleen Brown offer her own comprehensive vision for the state of California, she proudly cites the confident dreams of a past "wise leader," former Governor Pat Brown, her father. Not only does former Mayor, now United States Senator, Dianne Feinstein advocate increased national funding for AIDS research and education, she recalls the pain of losing friends and colleagues to the deadly disease and her pride in appropriating the first public funding for AIDS services and education. Not only does state Senator Diane Watson detail the "horrifying figures and statistics" on crack cocaine use, she helps us to understand the psychological and social traps that cause "so many young black people to stifle development of positive self-esteem." Not only does Assemblywoman Delaine Eastin address the budget crisis in higher education, she shares how the political turbulence of the 1960s shaped her passion for public service and her disdain for the "greed is good" philosophy of the 1980s. The commitment of these women goes far beyond the realms of politics—they have a personal stake in the issues that they are fighting for.

Sometimes this personal perspective means recognizing a problem and creating a new issue. One maxim of the women's movement has been that "the personal is political," and it is clear that many of the elected women in California have helped transform personal concerns into political issues. Former Supervisor Sandra Smoley, now the secretary of the

California Health and Welfare Agency, was one of the first leaders to go public with her fight against breast cancer. In her speech, she candidly shares the details of this battle—and displays a touching concern for women in less supportive circumstances.

Sometimes this personal perspective means casting off the protocols and pedestals of elected office and reaching out to another human being one-on-one. In compelling remarks to an audience of one, Sacramento Municipal Court Judge Alice Lytle speaks to a man brought before her court on charges of spousal abuse. She urges him to put aside his need to blame his wife and enter a diversion process rather than pursue a more divisive and rancorous jury trial.

Finally, several of the speeches call for a more inclusive public process, a value shared by many elected women. Associate Justice Joyce Kennard argues that the judiciary needs to be more representative of California's diverse population. In a thought-provoking speech on environmental racism, then-Assemblywoman Lucille Roybal-Allard, now a congresswoman, declares, "Our fight for survival transcends race and color boundaries. In order for us to accomplish our mission, local communities and communities of color and lower income *must be a part of the policymaking process.*"

As women have become a visible force in the policymaking process, they have literally changed the face of government. Yet until *California Women Speak*, there has been little written documentation of their public words.

Through the speeches that follow, 16 women display the policy expertise, personal commitment, empathy, and courage that have made them leaders in the state of California. Moreover, each has taken part in a political revolution: the entrance of women into politics.

Kate Karpilow, Ph.D.
Sacramento, California
February, 1994

Kate Karpilow is executive director of the California Elected Women's Association for Education and Research (CEWAER), the nation's oldest and largest non-profit association of elected women.

California Women Speak

Barbara Boxer

Barbara Boxer's college studies in economics were followed by several years as a stockbroker and economics researcher. A stint on a local newspaper, *Pacific Sun*, brought her an award for investigative reporting. In 1976, she was elected to the Marin County Board of Supervisors, and she became the first woman president of the board.

After serving six years on the Board of Supervisors, Barbara Boxer was elected to Congress representing the San Francisco Bay Area, and has been continuously in office since 1983. Her principal issues have been reform in military and government spending, AIDS research, women's and children's needs and protection of the environment. She initiated legislation to stop the slaughter of dolphins and to end driftnet fishing that has "strip-mined" marine resources. Her Dolphin Protection Consumer Information Act to establish criteria for "dolphin-safe" tuna and the driftnet ban became law in 1990. Over 90 percent of the United States tuna industry now uses dolphin-safe practices.

Boxer has met with leaders in Asia, Europe and the Middle East to discuss international relations, foreign trade and human rights. She has argued against federal funding which supports oppressive regimes in Central America, South Africa and Asia. Her work for human rights and the environment has been honored by many groups: the Sierra Club, the Anti-Defamation League, the Leadership Conference on Civil Rights, the American Police Hall of Fame and the Human Rights Campaign Fund, among others.

In 1992, Boxer was elected to the United States Senate. Early in her term, Boxer introduced legislation to create a "one-stop-shop" Conversion Clearinghouse to help workers and businesses in areas hard hit by defense cuts and military base closures. She drafted legislation to retrain defense workers to assist with environmental clean-up of the bases closed.

Boxer founded the California Unity Working Group to encourage bipartisan cooperation in dealing with issues important to California's future.

Barbara Boxer

United States Senate

Barbara Boxer

[Speech given to the California Legislative Symposium of the Planning and
Conservation League, January 10, 1992.]

*T*oday as all of America focuses on a weak and faltering economy, I want to shatter
a myth—a myth that says you can't protect the environment and have a prospering economy.

This myth, handed down from Ronald Reagan to James Watt to John Sununu to Dan
Quayle, is easy to disprove. Look at Eastern Europe.

When the wall came down, we could hardly see those cities of old through all the soot
and smog and filth. It is hard to tell which is more rotten—the air, the soil, the water or the
economy in Eastern Europe.

The Bush-Quayle Administration, devoid of original ideas to jump-start the U.S.
economy, has removed its cloak of green, invoked the myth, and placed in its sights the
resources many of you here today have dedicated your lives to protecting: our wetlands and
our forests, our coasts and the Arctic National Wildlife Refuge, our energy savings programs,
and our endangered species.

Meanwhile, far away from the meeting rooms of Quayle's Council on Competitiveness,
we Californians have become more and more aware of how the quality of our lives relates not
only to the quality of our environment, but to our economic well-being.

We know that if we cut our forests down, there will be none left to manage and work;
if we destroy our ocean and coast with offshore drilling, we ruin two of our biggest industries
in California—tourism and fishing; if we're trapped every day in a traffic nightmare, we can't
be productive; if we don't clean up the hazards in our soil, our soil will be sterile; if we waste
precious water, our cities, suburbs, farms and public lands will all suffer, and if we can't
breathe, we can't work.

These issues, once viewed in isolation from one another, are now more clearly
understood to be part of a larger issue—how to ensure our economic and social well-being
within the natural limits imposed by our environment.

Californians are often on the cutting edge in this comprehensive approach to the
environment and don't buy into the myth that prosperity and environmental protection are
at odds with each other.

Congress, unfortunately, far too often helps to perpetuate the myth.

—At the Administration's urging, as well as the oil companies' and the developers', 168 members of the House of Representatives have signed onto the Hayes-Breaux wetlands legislation that would eliminate over half of the nation's wetlands.

—At the Administration's urging, Congress turned its back on the environment and gave the President fast-track authority for the U.S.-Mexico Free Trade and GATT treaties.

—At the Administrations's urging, as well as the automakers', many in Congress have turned their backs on the single most important energy conservation need in America—raising automobile fuel economy standards.

—At the Administration's urging, as well as the oil companies', over half of the U.S. Senate sits poised to turn the Arctic National Wildlife Refuge (ANWR) into the next Prudhoe Bay.

In fact, some elected officials from our state would sell out on ANWR for a short-term reprieve for California's coast.

You need a senator who will never sell out the environment.

I'm not just another vote for the environment: I'm a fighter—an advocate. And I can change the way the U.S. Senate looks at the environment, to make them understand that a strong environment is vital to a prosperous America.

Let me tell you about some of the issues of tremendous concern to me.

I am incensed about the continued federal assault on California's wetlands. The state has already lost an incredible 91 percent of its historical wetlands.

Currently, less than a half-million acres of wetlands are left in California. San Francisco Bay, for example, is half the size it was just fifty years ago.

In Southern California, the 220-acre Biona wetlands are the last remaining major wetlands in all of Los Angeles County. They were once ten times that size.

The destruction of wetlands leads to economic ruin in the fishing industry, degradation of water quality, loss of critical waterfowl habitat, loss of critical flood control, and destruction of visual resources important to tourism.

For eight painfully long years, the Reagan-Bush Administration eliminated, diluted, and ignored vital wetlands regulations. And now the Bush Administration and the Quayle Council on Competitiveness have launched a sneak attack on wetlands protections.

As the recent EPA assessment of the Administration's proposal confirms, the new Bush-Quayle definition of wetlands could eliminate over 50 percent of our nation's remaining wetlands.

I have vehemently opposed the Administration's attempts to reclassify wetlands, as well as the Hayes-Breaux legislation that would implement much of that proposal.

In that last session of Congress, I authored a California congressional delegation letter to all members of Congress urging them to withdraw their support of the Hayes-Breaux legislation and to oppose the Administration's wetlands proposals.

Two members of Congress have withdrawn their support of the bill since my letter went out, and the letter is currently used as an education and lobbying tool by the environmental community.

Today I am announcing legislation that would hold President Bush to the "no-net-loss" wetlands pledge he made to the nation. In a speech to Ducks Unlimited on June 8th of 1989—one month after the 1989 wetlands manual had taken effect—President Bush pledged that he would keep his campaign promise on wetlands.

My legislation will define wetlands according to the 1989 wetlands manual—just as they were defined the day he made his pledge—and it will express the intent of Congress to support our President's promise that no more wetlands will be lost under that definition.

The wetlands issue is a good example of the extent to which the Administration buys into the myth. Another example is the fast-track authority the President sought and received from Congress for the U.S.-Mexico Trade Agreement and the General Agreement on Tariffs and Trade, or GATT as it is commonly known.

Fast-track authority allows the President to negotiate a treaty and get a speedy up-or-down vote from Congress without any opportunity for amendment.

I believed that Mexico's dismal environmental practices could one day supersede our nation's environmental regulations. Further, I believed that the environmental dangers of fast-track were far too great to put this sort of faith in the Administration.

Frankly, this was a tough vote from a California perspective, but I don't duck tough votes. I actively opposed fast-track.

However, Mexico promised to strengthen environmental protection and President Bush finally convinced a slim majority in Congress that the nation's right to safeguard the environment would be preserved under any free trade agreement.

Unfortunately, my fears were justified. The trouble has already begun.

Mexico has challenged a U.S. dolphin protection law and has been upheld by a GATT dispute panel. That panel held that the U.S. cannot regulate the protection of species outside the U.S. territorial jurisdiction—placing the Endangered Species Act, the Marine Mammal Protection Act, and other conservation efforts in extreme jeopardy.

In response, I authored a letter to President Bush and U.S. Trade Representative Carla Hills—signed by 62 of my colleagues—strongly supporting the right of every nation to enact laws to achieve worldwide conservation goals.

This effort has helped to prompt media attention, congressional hearings, and increased congressional awareness of the dangers of handing the Administration a blank check on trade.

Thanks to all of this attention and the political fallout, Mexico—which desperately wants a trade agreement—has yet to ask for the adoption of the ruling by the GATT participants.

Congressman Pete Stark and I have now introduced a resolution that urges the president to oppose any action under GATT which impinges on our ability to protect the environment worldwide.

GATT is pretty arcane stuff, but let me explain one very local impact to California. If the version of GATT currently under consideration is adopted, there will be no more Proposition 65. This could leave us powerless to protect ourselves from pesticides currently outlawed in California. That is why I am continuing to sound a warning to all who will listen. Likewise, I am continuing to spread the word about why it makes sense to reduce our energy consumption and clean up our energy sources.

The Bush Administration has attacked or ignored almost every progressive energy measure, including conservation, alternative and renewable energy, preserving the Arctic National Wildlife Refuge, and protection of our coasts.

The myth holds these are bad for the economy. The truth is that as we approach the 21st century, our country's economic survival depends on an energy policy emphasizing conservation, renewable resources, and alternative non-polluting fuels.

Look what happened at Chernobyl. Was that good for the Soviet economy? Given George Bush and Dan Quayle's support for nuclear energy, you would think so.

I have been a consistent supporter of energy conservation and environmentally safe, alternative energy—both for our environment and our economy.

I have testified and co-sponsored legislation for solar tax credits, and have promoted increased funding for alternative energy and transportation systems as a catalyst for kicking our nation's dependency on oil and boosting our economy.

One example of how energy conservation is good for the economy is home weatherization. Every 100 million dollars spent on home weatherization creates over 6,000 jobs.

The principal energy challenge for California is the motor vehicle. Trucks and cars account for over one half of the petroleum used in California.

These vehicles are also directly responsible for approximately 40 percent of California's carbon dioxide—the primary greenhouse gas.

I am the author of automobile fuel-economy legislation endorsed by the spectrum of environmental and energy conservation groups and enjoying the widest support of any such bill in the House of Representatives. It calls for foreign and domestic automakers to increase the fuel economy of their vehicles, enabling American drivers to enjoy 45 mile-per-gallon efficiency by 2001.

Energy and environmental experts recognize that increasing fuel economy is the fastest and greatest step we could take as a nation to reduce our dependency on oil, as well as to reduce carbon dioxide emissions.

We must press for increased fuel economy standards not only for environmental reasons, however, but to get our domestic auto industry competitive again. Since the OPEC oil embargo and the Japanese auto industry first caught Detroit off guard in the early '70s, American auto workers have paid the price for status quo management. Without increased fuel economy standards, the next big oil shock could find us calling AAA for a disabled American car economy.

Further, our dependence on foreign oil is fueling our trade imbalance. Every year Bush has been in office, imported oil has accounted for an increasingly higher percentage of our total trade deficit. In 1992, oil imports will account for over 46 billion dollars of our deficit, or 67 percent of the overall deficit.

Jobs. Health. The economy. All of these will improve with an environmentally sound energy policy and when we free ourselves from our oil dependence.

In contrast to President Bush and others who have called for more drilling off the California coast and in the Arctic National Wildlife Refuge, I authored the National Ocean Protection Act, which would ban offshore drilling off the Pacific and Atlantic coasts.

With this bill, I brought together the first bi-coastal coalition in Congress to keep the oil companies and their drilling rigs off our shores.

It got their attention. The oil industry took out ads in most of America's major newspapers attacking my bill.

—They don't want Americans to understand that if we drilled every drop of oil off the California coast we would get all of 90 days' worth—and that's it.

—They don't want the American public to know that without an energy policy we are headed down a path of increased trade deficits, dirty air, and dependence on oil tyrants.

—They don't want people to know that my automobile fuel-economy legislation would save six times the oil that lies off all the protected areas in my National Ocean Protection Act.

So they play to people's fears. They paint the issues as jobs versus the environment, or the economy versus the environment. But we know that the truth is that if we don't preserve our natural resources, our natural resources can't possibly preserve us.

For instance, the Administration wants the nation to believe that protecting our forests will cost jobs. We know that protecting our forests will sustain jobs. That is why I am backing comprehensive legislation (H.R. 3432) introduced by Congressman James McDermott that will protect our ancient forests and threatened watersheds—including our Sierras, that also provides economic assistance for community development and export assistance for the export of finished timber products.

Protecting our water resources also makes the greatest economic and environmental sense. That is why I am a co-sponsor of the Miller-Bradley Central Valley Restoration legislation.

So it is up to all of us to tell the truth about offshore oil drilling, about an energy policy, about wetlands, about forests, about the California desert, about water, about air, and about all the environmental issues we face. It is up to us to shatter the myth once and for all that a prosperous America must ignore its environment.

To the contrary, if we don't act now on all these critical environmental issues, we'll not only destroy America's environment and hurt our economy, we will destroy America's soul.

Thank you for the work you do.

Dianne Feinstein

Dianne Feinstein graduated from the Convent of the Sacred Heart High School in San Francisco in 1951 and from Stanford University in 1955, where she majored in history and was vice president of the student body. She began her career in public service in 1961 as a member of the California Women's Board of Terms and Parole where, for five years as an appointee of then-Governor Edmund G. "Pat" Brown, she set sentences and granted paroles to women convicted of felonies in California. In the late sixties, she headed a local committee urging reform of county jails, and served as a member of the San Francisco Committee on Crime.

She first ran for public office in 1969, seeking city-wide election to the City and County Board of Supervisors. Surprising everyone, she received the highest number of votes of all the candidates running for the five seats. By tradition as the highest vote-getter, she became president of the board—a position she won again in 1974 and 1978.

After serving nine years on the Board of Supervisors, she was elected by her colleagues to serve as the 35th mayor of San Francisco in the wake of the assassination of George Moscone. Upon finishing the final year of Mayor Moscone's four-year term, she was elected by the people to a full four-year term in 1979, and in 1983 won a second term by 81 percent of the vote.

During her ten years as mayor, she added more than 300 police officers and cut crime 27 percent. She created an urban conservation corps to teach job skills, applied modern management techniques to the city budget and was named the nation's most effective mayor. She was an advocate for child care programs, affordable housing, and trade and cultural links with Asian nations. The San Francisco program for treatment and prevention of AIDS became a national model.

In 1990, she won a contested Democratic primary and became the first woman major-party candidate for governor in California history. She lost the general election to Pete Wilson by less than 4 percent of the vote. In 1992 she was elected to the United States Senate. She is running for re-election in 1994 for her first full six-year term.

Her public service has been honored by many academic, religious and community organizations.

Dianne Feinstein

United States Senate

Dianne Feinstein

["A Woman for all Reasons," speech given to Women's Leadership Council,
Harbortown Marina Resort, Ventura Harbor, California, May 9, 1992.]

(This speech refers to the Los Angeles riots of 1992 which followed the verdict in the Rodney King
case against the Los Angeles Police Department officers involved in his arrest.)

On Saturday I toured the devastated areas of Los Angeles and saw firsthand the enormity of the damage.

We traveled through Inglewood, Watts, Compton, South Central, Crenshaw, Koreatown, the Pico Alvarado area and downtown.

I was driven by a man who operates three small restaurants in the area and by the president of the largest supermarket chain in the area.

The small businessman did not sustain losses; the supermarket chain had several of its stores burned to the ground and the remainder looted.

That evening, when I returned to San Francisco, I was numbed by the overwhelming impact of what I had seen.

So many questions crossed my mind:

Why would they kill others with such hate?

Why would people burn the businesses in their own area?

Why haven't the lessons from the Watts riot of '65 been learned?

These are big questions and the answers elusive.

Alienation, frustration and failure were lessons from Watts in 1965 left unheeded.

Two verdicts in the criminal courts provided the spark to set off the largest incidence of civil hostility in peacetime America's history.

Reverend Cecil Murray, pastor of Los Angeles' First AME Church, the oldest black congregation in that city, says it this way:

"People don't burn down a city over a singular event.

They burn down a city over 200 years of events.

...For the vast one-third below the poverty line, things
are worse than ever. You can't sustain yourself on
$6,000 a year, $15,000 a year, or $18,000 a year.

...We had 15 years of hope and then the reaction set in
—Nixon, Reagan, Bush, trickle down and benign neglect.

...You try to produce, you run across redlining, you run
across insurance "no can get," you run across bank loans
"no can get." We own nothing. And you want to know
why the rage?

Add to this the frustrations and failures—drugs, gangs, and guns—and then the spark of injustices done in a major way which said, "If you're black there is no justice."

First Latasha Harlins, and then Rodney King, and *boom*! The insurrection began.

And so the question is, "How do we pick up the pieces, and where do we go from here?"

I believe that we need to be able to encourage business to start up and ease the great difficulty for those who might be willing to reinvest in the destroyed commercial strips throughout the troubled areas of Los Angeles.

To that end I would propose:

1) The immediate creation of strong enterprise zones. I believe very strongly we need to provide tax incentives to businesses that employ people in inner cities, including credits for wages, health care and R & D, and capital gains exemptions.

2) The creation of private community reinvestment banks which would provide low-interest loans to small businesses based on the ability of the individuals involved to succeed with no redlining.

Throughout the '80s the American economy was characterized by a pattern of overspending and underinvesting.

Today we find too much debt wherever we look, be it in the government, or in the corporate sectors, or with many individuals. Much of this was created by the supply-side policies of the 80s that took us from being the world's largest creditor nation to the world's largest debtor in a few years.

Now, with a trillion and a half dollars owed by the federal government, a substantial part of our budget (approximately $100 billion a year) is used for interest and debt repayment rather than for America's critical needs.

Expanded military spending ($1.45 trillion over 5 years) and a low tax policy for the most wealthy not only hurt the middle class, but also made us less competitive as a nation as we underinvested in infrastructure, education, and training.

The tax cuts were trickle up, not trickle down.

There are two ways of stimulating the economy in the short-term. The first is through monetary policy. Interest rates were lowered nine times in 1991, and the federal funds rate has already been lowered in 1992.

There are some indications that this change may begin to move the economy. But even lower interest rates don't help much in critical areas like commercial and housing development if banks won't or can't lend.

The second way of jump-starting the economy is through fiscal policy. Many in Washington are hesitant to follow this route for fear of exacerbating the budget deficit.

But California has lost 660,000 jobs within the last 15 months, according to the Center for the Continuing Study of the California Economy in Palo Alto.

That's the equivalent of every man, woman, and child in the county of Ventura, or San Mateo, or San Joaquin, or Fresno—or in the cities of Anaheim, Bakersfield and Riverside *combined*. And add to this aerospace and defense job losses we know are coming.

I was a mayor during the 1980s. I saw every single program that allowed us on the local level to care—cut, slashed, and decimated.

I saw the *Comprehensive Employment Training Act (CETA)* which allowed cities to train the unemployed—decimated.

I saw the *Economic Development Administration* which built the container facilities and made Oakland competitive as one of the great ports of this state—ended.

I saw the *Urban Development Action Grant Program* which leveraged the private sector to provide jobs by building economic facilities such as the great produce market which saved 6,000 jobs for the city of Los Angeles—ended.

I saw them slash all capital and operating grants to cities that ran rail systems like we did, so that we would have to take money from police and fire to run transit systems, showing that they didn't care whether the trains or buses ran on time.

I saw *revenue sharing ended*.

I saw *affordable housing programs cut*. Today, it's virtually impossible to build housing for the poor and needy. And, yes, today it's nearly impossible to build housing even for seniors.

I saw every city in this nation, and particularly in this state which is a Proposition 13 state, get tighter and tighter in its budget—less able to care, less able to produce programs to abate gangs, to fight drugs, to clean up streets, prevent crime.

We were told there would be 30 million new jobs. In California we've lost over 5 percent of our job base in the last 15 months alone.

Our state is growing, 700,000 to 1,000,000 people a year, and we can't employ our own people. We need to create 250,000 new jobs a year just remain even; instead we've lost three times that.

Today, in the president's budget there is $100 billion for the **defense of Europe** in NATO. There are 150,000 American troops sent to defend Europe.

We spend more today for the defense of Germany than Germany does itself. We spend more for Korea's defense than Korea spends. More for Japan's defense than Japan spends.

I say the time has come **for Europe, for Korea, and for Japan to pay for their own defense.** We should return those monies home and invest them in America again.

Today, I want to make two points. I hope these are two points that are really very clear already to everyone in this room.

The first is that *we woman have had to fight for everything we've gotten in life*.

And the second is that *two percent representation in the U.S. Senate is not enough*.

To dramatize that latter point, just consider:

What would men do if the United States Senate was 98 women and two men today? Indeed.

I say we need to rise and do **just that same thing!**

I want to ask each of you here to join me in that fight.

And I want to point out, candidly and clearly, that it is not going to be an easy fight.

I am running to retire an incumbent Republican, John Seymour, from the United States Senate. But I believe that the Republicans will do everything they possibly can to keep me from getting there. So I'm asking for your help.

As I said, we have always had to fight for equality.

In 1920, women marched for the right to vote. And we fought to be able to go to school, and later, to own property. It was only because we took to the streets and marched for that vote.

And a month ago in Washington, 700,000 strong of us, men and women, marched for the right to control our own reproductive systems.

I remember looking for a job before the 1964 Civil Rights Bill was passed. I remember being often passed over by men with less of a résumé, less education than I had. And yet, until Title VII of the 1964 Civil Rights Act, it was commonplace to discriminate against a woman for employment.

Since the 1964 Civil Rights Act, a woman can, in fact, sue for damages, if she proves she was discriminated against on the basis of her sex for employment.

Thirty years ago we were one-third of the work force. Today, we are the majority of the work force.

And yet, less than 2.9 percent of us are in senior executive or corporate positions in this nation. A subtle but firm glass ceiling prevents us from getting there. We need to shatter that glass ceiling.

And now the 1991 Civil Rights Act gives women the opportunity to sue for damages if they are passed over for a promotion *on the basis of sex alone*. The shattering will begin.

We need to remember that despite the fact that we are a majority of the work force, and a majority of the voting public in this country, in many ways our rights seem to be diminishing instead of expanding.

For example, **the Equal Rights Amendment**—a simple 24-word amendment that would guarantee us equal treatment under law—in credit, in the military, in criminal sentencing—the same laws would apply to us that apply to men.

Once the ERA was on the *front* burner, close to ratification, but **now** it's on the *back* burner and even expunged from the Republican platform.

For example, **control of our reproductive systems**. I set sentences in California when abortion was illegal thirty years ago. I set the sentences for five years, of women convicted of illegal abortion in this state.

I read the case studies of the back alley abortionists. Of the morbidity. Of the mortality. Of the suicides that took place.

We **cannot** go back thirty years!

The Supreme Court recently started hearing *Planned Parenthood v. Casey*, the case challenging the anti-abortion law in Pennsylvania.

This is the **final warning** for all of us who believe the Constitution should protect the right to privacy.

We sounded the **first alarm** when the courts began dismantling the fundamental principle of *Roe v. Wade* with the **Webster case** of 1989.

Hundreds of thousands marched in the streets, but anti-choice judges dominate our federal courts.

We sounded **another alarm** as George Bush, a president absolutely committed to making abortion illegal again, **gagged doctors** and family planning counselors from discussing abortion, **but** we didn't have enough pro-choice votes in Congress to overturn Bush's veto.

And we have watched in angry disbelief as religious extremists terrorize young women and destroy family planning clinics with arson and vandalism around the country.

But you can't stop terrorism when the encouragement comes from the top. Attorneys for the Bush Administration, using taxpayer funds, stepped in to argue in favor of allowing these extremists to continue to close clinics any way they could.

And now we will watch as the Supreme Court quite probably removes the last vestiges of constitutional protection for safe and legal abortion in this country with the *Planned Parenthood* case.

Make no mistake about the seriousness of this case: *Planned Parenthood v. Casey* marks the critical turning point in the Court's reversal of *Roe v. Wade*. If the Court upholds any part of the Pennsylvania law's restrictions, *Roe* will be history.

Thirteen states are prepared to ban abortion. Dozens of others will make abortions so difficult to obtain that it may as well be illegal. Women died by the thousands before *Roe v. Wade* and they will die again when *Roe* is gone.

The only course of action left to us is to ensure that the *Freedom of Choice Act*, which codifies the principles in *Roe v. Wade*, becomes the law of this nation.

We can only do that with a **pro-choice president** and a pro-choice Congress. We need at least **17 to 20** new pro-choice members in the U.S. Senate and even more in the House to have a veto-proof majority.

This is the final alarm. Our vote is all we have left to protect our right to choose. Let us use it wisely and well.

Another example. Today we're a majority of the work force. Most of us in the United States work force are married—and most have children. The U.S. is the **only** major industrial power on Earth that denies a worker the opportunity to take care of a sick child or a sick parent.

And family and medical leave was vetoed by the president. It will be vetoed by the president again.

It must be passed.

Child care and family medical leave are not social niceties—they are economic necessities to working women with families.

To that end we have proposed a 5-year 'Invest in America' program, using our dollars here at home to build our schools, repair our roads, build transportation systems—putting people back to work in this country, and caring about our inner cities once again.

I believe very strongly that 2 percent representation isn't enough to **move** a women's agenda.

Let me suggest to you the 10 critical points of our women's agenda for the '90s.

The first part of that agenda is to guarantee *freedom of choice* and eliminate the gag law for all time.

Second, provide *equal rights under the law* so that we get the same treatment as men.

Third, demand *equal pay for equal work*, so that instead of making $.68 for the $1.00 that a man makes for the same job, we make an equal amount for the same job.

Fourth, enact *unpaid medical and family leave* for working women so that a working woman can take care of a critically ill child or a critically ill parent.

Fifth, mandate *employer supported child care*. It's necessary to keep workers on the job.

Sixth, *shatter the glass ceiling*. Today, *2.9 percent* of America's senior executives are women.

By the year 2000 women must take their places boldly in the board rooms and among the senior executives of this nation. We must use the 1991 Civil Rights Act to accomplish this.

Seventh, achieve *women's health equity*.

We're not going to be second-class citizens when it comes to health care ever again.

Eighth, *strengthen and enforce child support—the largest single reason that one out of four of our children is raised in poverty today* is the absence of child support.

And we can amend the federal child support law to prevent someone running from the state to avoid paying child support.

Ninth, *end **all** discrimination and sexual harassment* in the workplace, all *battering and domestic violence* in the homeplace.

And finally, elect more women to public office.

We've got a lot of work ahead of us.

I hope you will take seriously our biggest fund-raising event of the primary. There will be 500 simultaneous house parties held across the state. There's a notice about these house parties marked ABC.

If you could have a house party, just a coffee, invite some of your friends in who could contribute $20 or $30 or $40 to this campaign—the effort will clearly bring in hundreds of thousands of dollars.

If you believe that this is an important agenda—

If you believe that I can make a difference—that I will stand up for what I say to you today—that I will advocate for change that is positive to men, to women, to children in this room—then I need your support.

Remember, 2 percent is not enough and we **can make a difference**.

I want just to end with one quote from the final line in Susan Faludi's book, *Backlash*:

> "Whatever new obstacles are mounted against the future march towards equality—whatever new myths invented, penalties levied, opportunities rescinded, or degradation imposed, no one can ever take from the American woman the justice of her cause."

[What follows is an exerpt of a speech given to MECLA (Municipal Elections Committee of Los Angeles) Biltmore Hotel, Tiffany Room, Los Angeles, April 11, 1992.]

Thank you for inviting me to this very important forum today.

It's hard to believe that I have been campaigning now for three years.

As I've traveled up and down this great state I have found that forums like this are my best opportunity to speak directly to the people.

So often, positions about which I feel strongly are not carried by the media. As we are witnessing in the presidential campaigns, issues of substance are often dwarfed by the media's preoccupation with sensational headlines.

This has been particularly true for me, I believe, because I'm a woman. The "old-boys" who run the media seem to hold women to very different standards. Perhaps that's part of the reason there are only two women in the United States Senate.

I'll give you an example of what I mean. When I debated Pete Wilson in the governor's race, the Los Angeles Times declared the debate to be a virtual tie. However, they felt that he **looked** more like a governor. I'll give you another example. In my campaign for governor, I repeatedly called for the signing of what would become AB-101 [legislation banning discrimination based on sexual orientation]. When I announced as a candidate, when I addressed the State Democratic Convention, and when I attended literally scores of functions around the state, I pledged to sign that legislation. But did you ever hear or read of this in the mainstream media? No. Although it was in vain, they thought trying to dig up something personally negative about me or my husband was more important to the voters.

So, for those of you who don't know my record, let me briefly review some of the highlights. I might add they are highlights of which I am proud.

When I first campaigned for public office back in the '60s, I was alone in seeking the support of the gay and lesbian community. I went to a group called the Society for Individual Rights down on Sixth Street. I still remember walking up those stairs. That night, I met people who would become friends for life. One of them was Jim Foster. I'm sure some of you know of him. He made history in 1972 at the Democratic National Convention in Miami where he gave a speech calling for an end to the oppression of gay people.

Jim and I went to the next convention in 1976. I was on the Rules Committee that year and Jim, along with other friends, helped me as I fought for the inclusion of a gay rights plank in the party platform. And later, when I was mayor, he was my first appointment to San Francisco's newly formed Health Commission. Tragically, that brilliant life was cut short. As with so many of my dear friends, he was lost to AIDS.

When I won the first election to the Board of Supervisors in 1969, I kept my promise and began work on issues that we talked about that night. *I am proud to say that I was the author of pioneering legislation which prohibited discrimination on the basis of sexual orientation.*

Back in the days when supervisors were given only one staff person, I hired an openly gay man as my aide. I believe I was the first elected official in the country to do so. He was with me that awful day when Harvey Milk was shot in the cubicle next to mine. And he was by my side as we walked over from the legislative side of City Hall to the executive side where I had to make that terrible announcement.

As mayor, I continued my commitment to empower the community, and brought lesbians and gay men into city government in unprecedented numbers. I appointed openly gay people to important city boards and commissions including police, health, human rights, and many others. And I hired more people onto the mayor's staff. Also, I regularly held meetings, (they were problem-solving sessions really) with a broad group of community representatives. The community was so proud. It was blossoming and just coming into its own at that time.

It was at one of those meetings, in 1981, that activists told me of rumors of a so-called "gay cancer." I instructed our director of public health to investigate immediately. When he did, he confirmed that New York and the Centers for Disease Control in Atlanta were reporting a new and growing phenomenon which included those unusual purple lesions, which by now have become all too familiar.

Little did any of us know the extent of the epidemic which was about to occur. That first year, I appropriated funding for AIDS services and education. *I believe it was the first public funding for AIDS anywhere.*

When I was mayor, San Francisco spent more money for AIDS than all other cities in the country combined. For most years of the epidemic, we also spent more than the state of California. During my administration, we opened the nation's first AIDS wards, conducted important research, created a full spectrum of services, facilitated clinical drug trials at our county hospital, and quickly adopted tough anti-discrimination measures.

The AIDS model developed in San Francisco is testimony to the courage and vision of the gay and lesbian community. Working with the community to develop that model remains one of my proudest achievements. *Together we made history.*

However, I must tell you, failing to beat AIDS was one of my most profound disappointments. As chair of the U.S. Conference of Mayors, I spearheaded an intensive lobbying effort with Congress. *But a mayor is limited in what she can do.*

As a United States senator, I will be able to do what I could not do as mayor. I'll do everything possible to see that federal funding reaches an adequate level and is well-spent. *Every dollar must have maximum impact on increasing our ability to find a cure.*

As a United States senator, *I will fight to move funding for AIDS research and education to the forefront of the American political agenda.*

And as a United States senator, *I will fight until there is a cure.*

I was there at the beginning of the AIDS epidemic. I want very much to be there at its end.

Nancy Pelosi

 $\mathcal{N}$ ancy Pelosi comes from a strong family tradition of public service. Her father, Thomas D'Alesandro, Jr., served as mayor of Baltimore after representing the city for a decade in Congress, where he served, as his daughter now does, on the Appropriations Committee. Her brother, Thomas III, also served as mayor of Baltimore.

Pelosi brings to her office experience gained through years of work in the community and the Democratic Party, including service as state chair of the California Democratic Party.

In 1987, Pelosi was elected to represent San Francisco in Congress. She serves on the House Appropriations Committee and the House Committee on Standards of Official Conduct (Ethics). She was elected as Northern California Democratic Whip and serves on the Executive Committee of the Democratic Study Group. She chairs the Congressional Working Group on China.

In the field of human rights, Congresswoman Pelosi has championed the cause of democracy in China, introducing legislation to protect Chinese students from forcible return to China after the Tiananmen Square massacre. She also introduced legislation conditioning most-favored-nation trade status for China on improvements in the treatment of its citizens.

On the issue of housing, Congresswoman Pelosi introduced bills which became law to preserve the nation's existing supply of housing for low-income families and to establish programs to prevent homelessness among people with AIDS.

In the area of health care, Pelosi has introduced several bills that have become law: to ensure continued health care for people forced to leave their jobs due to a disability; to authorize money for innovative health programs in the fight against AIDS; and to improve prenatal care for low-income families.

As part of her efforts to strengthen environmental protection, Pelosi authored a law requiring the World Bank and other multinational banks to complete environmental assessments on projects prior to United States approval of loans.

Nancy Pelosi

United States House of Representatives
8th Congressional District

Nancy Pelosi

[Speeches given in the House of Representatives.]

[March 31, 1992]

*M*r. Speaker, I am pleased to take part in this special order today on the creation of a new radio service for the people of China and Southeast Asia. Like Radio Free Europe, which was instrumental in opening up the Iron Curtain, Radio Free China and Radio Free Asia would supply listeners behind the Bamboo Curtain with uncensored news and commentary.

Let me begin my remarks by paying special tribute to Congresswoman Helen Bentley and Congressman John Porter for their work on this issue and their efforts in convening this special order.

I believe that American foreign policy lacks consistency. While I understand the need for variation in our approach to different cultures, our foreign policy should be guided by underlying principles which do not vary: democratic reform, the protection of human rights, fair and open trade, weapons accountability.

Human rights abuses have always been of more paramount concern to the United States when they have involved Europeans. When they have occurred in Asia or in Latin America, for example, the United States has paid little more than lip service to them. Recall, for example, the lukewarm United States response to the Cambodian genocide under Pol Pot and to recurring atrocities in East Timor. Consider the longstanding United States policy of support for Chilean dictator Augusto Pinochet despite ample evidence of hideous human rights abuses by officials of his government. The list goes on.

As chair of the Congressional Working Group on China, I have advocated for consistency in our foreign policy—if it was our policy to condition MFN [most-favored-nation status] for the Soviet Union, then it should be our policy to condition the same MFN for China. If we thought it worthwhile to fund radio transmissions into Eastern Europe, then we should fund them into China and Tibet. If we considered Europeans worthy of our efforts to ensure their basic freedoms, then we should extend the same effort to Asians.

Mr. Speaker, this country has been the cause of some of the greatest innovations of our age, but none is as important as our dedication to the protection of basic human freedoms. This forms the basis of our democracy and provides our most important export. The protections provided for in our Bill of Rights and the spirit of freedom enshrined in our

Declaration of Independence are not uniquely American. They strike a chord in Europe, Asia, Latin America and Africa. They have spawned momentous changes in the Soviet Union, in Argentina, Chile, parts of Africa and Asia.

We must encourage these changes. Radio Free Asia and Radio Free China would give us a direct communications link to the people of China and Southeast Asia. In a censored society, information becomes a potent catalyst for change. Radio Free Asia and China are opportunities that should not be squandered.

With opportunity, however, comes responsibility. If we decide to spend the $100 million on Radio Free China that Mr. Porter advocates, then we must be willing to support the people who respond to our pro-democratic message. Although this body has stood steadfastly behind those who, responding to Voice of America, were arrested in Tiananmen Square nearly three years ago, the administration has decided that continuing its relationship with the Beijing regime is more important than demanding the release of pro-democracy advocates.

So, Mr. Speaker, I fully support the efforts of Mr. Porter and Mrs. Bentley to establish a radio service for the people of Asia—with one proviso—that we not only send the message of freedom, but also support those who respond to it. For this is the real test of our commitment to democracy and human rights.

. . .

[June 3, 1992]

Mr. Speaker, this week the third anniversary of the Tiananmen Square massacre will be observed. On the eve of that observation, the president of the United States has sent a request to the Congress to request a special waiver for favorable trade treatment for the People's Republic of China, thereby rewarding the butchers of Beijing.

Our colleague in the House of Representatives, the gentlemen from Ohio [Mr. Pease], is introducing legislation today to condition most-favored nation status for China on improvement in human rights conditions there, and on the stopping of the proliferation of nuclear weapons, and stopping the barriers of our trade going into China. This legislation is still necessary because just a couple of weeks ago, the Chinese tested a megaton bomb, 70 times more powerful than what was dropped on Hiroshima. China continues trade barriers. The trade deficit for this year for the first quarter is higher than the first quarter of last year. And the abuses of human rights and repression in China continue. That is why the legislation is still needed.

I believe we will win this time because the legislation offered by the gentleman from Ohio [Mr. Pease] is very targeted. It will revoke most-favored nation status on para-state or state-run industries.

I urge our colleagues who are concerned about these issues to join in co-sponsoring the legislation. This year I believe we can win and maybe the president of the United States will sign the legislation.

.   .   .

[July 21, 1992]

Mr. Speaker, I thank the chairman for yielding time to me, and I rise in support of the bill of the gentleman from Ohio [Mr. Pease] to condition most-favored nation status for China on improvements in human rights there, improvements in our trade relationship and in the area of nuclear proliferation.

I commend the gentleman from Illinois [Mr. Rostenkowski] and the gentleman from Florida [Mr. Gibbons] for their support of and commitment to prompt action on this legislation.

I want to pay special tribute to my colleague, the gentleman from Ohio [Mr. Pease], the author of this bill, whose commitment to workers' rights and human rights worldwide is well known. The gentleman from Ohio [Mr. Pease] in his opening remarks clearly set out what this bill does. In presenting this legislation he has created a solution to our policy impasse with China.

This bill encourages the role of private business in creating economic and political reform. It protects Hong Kong while isolating the hard-line regime in Beijing. It safeguards American manufacturing jobs and demands the responsible management of dangerous weapons, and it provides hope, hope for millions of Chinese who have fallen into disfavor with a regime that disavows their right to speak freely, to write, to worship, to dream.

We have all heard in the course of this debate, in the earlier legislation presented by the gentleman from New York [Mr. Solomon] why we have a need for this legislation, what the human rights situation is in China—and it is deplorable. We know what the trade situation is and we know what the nuclear proliferation treaty is.

Why is this legislation so important to the American people? Mr. Speaker, I believe it is necessary for our colleagues to join in giving the strongest possible vote to this legislation because of the serious trade imbalance that exists between our two countries. China has enjoyed since Tiananmen Square a $30 billion trade surplus with us. They have done this, and in addition they have profited from trans-shipments. That is when they say something is made in another country which is really made in China, to avoid our quotas. It is important to the American people because China has barriers to our products going into China. It is a large market indeed, if we could access it, but the Chinese have created barriers to our products going there, and the use of slave labor, forced labor, is well-known and well-documented. This is unfair to the American people.

Yes, this bill is about human rights, the human rights of political prisoners in China, human rights of all the people in China who cannot speak or worship freely. It is also about the human rights of American workers who are being deprived of the real opportunity our country could provide for them because of this administration's policies toward China.

By the end of this year, China will have probably, in the Bush administration, enjoyed a $50 billion surplus, and all the jobs that are implied in that. What does the government spend this money on? Mr. Speaker, largely it spends its money on weapons. According to numerous reports, the Chinese are buying sophisticated Russian weapons as fast as the cash-strapped republics, former republics of the Soviet Union, can sell them.

The gentleman from Ohio [Mr. Pease] referred to the megaton bomb that was tested, as did other speakers. The Chinese regime is building its military muscle and is using its trade surplus to pay for it. The hard currency provided by the trade surplus is also strengthening the regime in power. Their hard currency enables it to dominate the economy and therefore continue to repress its people politically.

Earlier I referred to an op-ed in the *New York Times* written by Bao Pu. Bao Tong is the person who was on trial today and was sentenced to seven years.

In China when we had the Tiananmen Square massacre, the soldiers who killed the students who were demonstrating peacefully each got a watch commending them for putting down the turmoil. Today the regime gave to this brave and courageous gentleman, who was a reformer who tried to warn the students about the coming of martial law, they gave him not a watch but seven years in prison. His son says in this article—which I commend to my colleagues for their reading, and I wish to submit for the Record—"Bao Tong's persistent efforts to grapple with seemingly clashing viewpoints and his personal sacrifice for a vision of a better future for the people of China exemplifies the kind of courage and strength respected by people everywhere."

Therefore, it is important to the American people for this legislation to pass and for it to become law. It is important because of American jobs, it is important because of fairness in our trade relationship with China—in that regard it is important because of the safety of the world. Strategically it is important for us not to have China buying up weapons and in turn selling them to unsafeguarded countries throughout the world, more specifically, Iran and Syria, who have been mentioned in similar legislation. It is important because of human rights and who we are as a people.

For two centuries this House has been a citadel for freedom, safeguarding against tyranny. I urge my colleagues to support this because of human rights in China and Tibet and also the human rights of American workers.

Lucille Roybal-Allard

$\mathscr{C}$ongresswoman Lucille Roybal-Allard was elected to represent California's 33rd Congressional District in 1992. She is the first Mexican-American woman elected to the United States House of Representatives. Recognizing her leadership abilities, her fellow Congree menbers elected her vice president of the freshman congressional class and vice president of the Congressional Hispanic Caucus.

Prior to her election to Congress, Lucille Roybal-Allard represented California's 56th Assembly District after winning a special election in May, 1987. Consistently re-elected by large margins, she represented the cities of Vernon, Maywood, Commerce, Bell Gardens, a large section of East Los Angeles, and, within the city of Los Angeles, portions of the downtown, Japanese, Chinese and Korean communities until 1992.

In the Assembly, Roybal-Allard sat on a number of influential committees including the Rules Committee and the Ways and Means Committee. She chaired the Ways and Means Subcommittee No. 1 on Health and Human Services. In charge of giving first approval for the budgets of state departments ranging from Corrections and Mental Health to Drug and Alcohol Programs, her subcommittee reviewed over $32 billion of combined state and federal funds annually while she was in the Assembly.

Roybal-Allard is a trailblazer on women's issues. She authored and won passage of laws that require the courts to take an individual's history of domestic violence into consideration during child-custody hearings. She negotiated an agreement with the Association of Obstetricians and Gynecologists to distribute free informational brochures to expectant mothers regarding Caesarean section procedures.

Roybal-Allard successfully carried a bill which entitled every community in the state to an environmental impact report before a toxic incinerator is built or expanded, a protection that was missing prior to her effort. The bill's passage came out of the East Los Angeles community's struggle against a proposed toxic waste incinerator in the nearby city of Vernon. This bill, along with her strong voting record on the environment, brought her the Sierra Club's Environmental Achievement Award.

Born and raised in Boyle Heights, Los Angeles, Lucille Roybal-Allard is the eldest daughter of former Congressman Edward Roybal and his wife Lucille Roybal. She attended Saint Mary's Catholic School and has a BA degree from UCLA.

Lucille Roybal-Allard

United States House of Representatives
33rd Congressional District

Lucille Roybal-Allard

["Protecting Southern California's Environment:
Living in the 1990s"]

*I*n keeping with today's theme, "Protecting Southern California's Environment: Living in the 1990s," I have been asked to address environmental issues from the perspective of minorities.

But before we proceed, let us reach a common understanding of the term "environment." For environment can mean different things to different people.

For example, environment to a mother in Beverly Hills may mean congestion on Rodeo Drive and dying trees on her street as a result of air pollution.

To a mother in East Los Angeles, environment may mean dirty streets in need of repair and a neighborhood encircled by heavy industry.

To still others it may mean our dying forests or polluted oceans and streams.

Therefore, for purposes of this presentation, let us reach a common accord by turning to Webster's definition of environment. "Environment is the aggregate of social and cultural conditions that influence the life of an individual or a community. It is the complex of physical, chemical, and biotic factors that act upon an organism or an ecological community and ultimately determines its form and survival."

The preceding [idea] clearly defines why each and every one of us is here today. For we are on a mission. That mission is one of survival.

The reality of our current situation is, we are past the stage of protecting our environment.

The fact is, we are now at the stage where we must save what has not already been destroyed and rebuild those areas that can be revived.

As evidenced by your presence here today and your proven dedication of the past, you know the time to act is now. For tomorrow may be entirely too late for some and the day after for all of us.

As you are aware, our air in Southern California is already the worst in the country; by 1992, Los Angeles County will be collecting more trash than there will be places to dump it; and according to the Little Hoover Commission, fourteen other California counties will run out of landfills in the next eight years. Nationally, the Environmental Protection Agency recently predicted most landfills throughout the United States will be filled by the rapidly approaching year 2000. All of which leads us to our purpose for being here today, which is to continue our mission to assure the survival of our environment.

However, this fight for survival is not a new struggle for poor and minority communities, communities such as Casmalia, Richmond, Martinez, Kettleman City, El Centro and East Los Angeles, just to name a few.

Our social and political institutions have negatively impacted these and other communities like them for decades. These institutions formed to protect citizens have threatened the health and quality of their lives by routinely permitting dangerous and unwanted projects to be built in their neighborhoods, and have ignored their repeated cries for help.

Such institutionalized disregard for the outcries of human life has necessitated the creation of a new term in our vocabulary: "environmental racism."

Although environmental racism has probably existed from the beginning of time, it wasn't until recently, when all neighborhoods, not just those in poor and minority communities, began to experience for themselves the terrible impact of garbage, pollution, and the dumping of hazardous waste, that others began joining the once lonely struggle for survival experienced for years by the poor and minority communities.

These new coalitions and cooperative efforts of communities working together to achieve a quality life will make it possible for all of us to emerge victorious.

The victory, however, will not be easily achieved.

The victory will take more than source reduction, recycling, and better technology.

The victory will require that we eliminate environmental racism by changing the attitudes and structures of our society to reflect what has always been true: "The survival of one group in society is dependent on the survival of all."

As a California legislator, I am convinced that we must begin by changing our policies and laws which encourage environmental racism and allow industries to exist and to operate without any regard or concern for the health and safety of the communities they impact—policies as exemplified by those advocated in a report prepared by Cerrell and Associates in 1983 for the California Waste Management Board.

The report recommended that communities which are economically depressed be given high priority and that officials and companies should look for lower socio-economic neighborhoods in which to locate undesirable projects—a policy which research has proven to be in effect nationwide.

Also our environmental laws need to be strengthened. As you know, they are riddled with so many loopholes, they protect even the worst polluter.

It is outrageous that environmental laws allow companies to violate the law and continuously endanger our health and safety, through their ability to operate, to expand their current facilities, and to build new facilities throughout the state of California.

Furthermore, it is outrageous our governor would veto my bill, AB411, which would have changed currently policy and required the Department of Health Services and allowed the AQMD [regional air quality management district] to deny permits if companies have a recurring history of health and safety violations. The time has come for people's lives to take priority over industry's bottom line.

The devastating effects of these policies are something with which my district is only too familiar. As a poor minority community, my district has for years been the dumping ground for unwanted projects in the state of California.

My district is the community where every major freeway crosses, and where a mass-burn garbage plant was allowed to operate for almost two years without a health risk assessment or a certified monitoring system.

Further, it is the district where the state's first commercial hazardous waste incinerator is proposed.

Although it is the first of its kind to be built in an urban area, the company which has been given all but its final permit to construct the incinerator has a long history of health and safety violations. Violations so severe that in spite of today's weak environmental laws, the company was forced to close its Garden Grove facility.

When agencies responsible, by law, for protecting our health and safety were asked why this company was granted these permits, and why they were allowed to come into our community, the response was they didn't have to consider the company's current performance record or history of violations when granting the permit under current law and regulations.

And with further disregard for the well-being of the men, women, and children of this community, permits were granted without the Department of Health Services, the AQMD, or even the Environmental Protection Agency requiring an Environmental Impact Report for this, the first hazardous waste incinerator of its kind in the state.

Although it is too late to have an impact in East Los Angeles, due to the governor's veto last year, I am happy to report that our struggle has not been in vain. For it produced my bill AB 58, which the governor signed into law this year. Now hazardous waste incinerators can no longer be permitted in the state of California without at least giving the people the minimum protection of an EIR.

The hazardous waste incinerator issue is a perfect example of environmental racism. Let me share a few insights with you. When the residents of my district came to me for help against this incinerator the first thing they asked was why? Why us again? Our community is already overburdened with unwanted and dangerous projects. We already fear for the lives of our children who we are told are potential victims of lead poisoning from automobile exhaust emissions because we are surrounded by freeways. Why, they pleaded, are they trying to destroy us?

Their questions were, of course, valid. But history has already taught us the answers. For my constituents are all too familiar with the policies of environmental racism.

This time, however, the community said enough is enough and was determined to fight back, no matter how long the odds. It was, they said, a matter of life or death. It was a matter of survival.

So they organized their community, and with people such as yourselves, who came into East Los Angeles not as rescuers, but as equal allies offering help and support, a project that would otherwise be built and operating today has been unable to obtain its final permit. And as far as the East Los Angeles community is concerned, it never will. For East Los Angeles is taking charge of its own community and determining is own destiny. And with the continued help and support of our allies we will succeed.

Strengthening and changing our laws and current policies will not be easy. As those of you who lobby in Sacramento know full well, our adversaries are a very strong and powerful industry.

Therefore, political activism is essential if we are going to attain a quality future for all of us. We must make our voices heard in Sacramento and in Washington, D.C. Together we must empower ourselves politically by electing more men and women who will fight on our behalf and by defeating those who ignore us.

Actions such as these will enable us to be heard when we speak as a group.

Our fight for survival transcends race and color boundaries. In order for us to accomplish our mission, local communities and communities of color and lower income must be a part of the policy-making process.

For if policies are to be fair and equitable, we must all, regardless of social or economic differences, share equally in the responsibility, the burden, and the benefits of our environmental survival.

I therefore challenge everyone in this room to work in unison with all communities to obtain positive environmental change.

For the full measure of success will never be realized unless we learn to work together as one community.

If we allow inequities to exist for any sector of our society, we will all be subjected to cruel limitations on the quality of our life and the fulfillment of our potential.

We must work together as a united force to win our fight for survival. Only then will we truly achieve a safer and healthier life in the 1990s.

Maxine Waters

*I*n November, 1990, Maxine Waters was elected to represent California's 29th Congressional District. She serves on the Committee on Banking, Finance and Urban Affairs, the Committee on Veterans' Affairs and the Democratic Caucus' Organization for Study and Review.

From 1976 to 1990, Congresswoman Waters served in the California State Assembly where she became the first woman in the state's history to be elected to chair the Assembly Democratic Caucus. Her legislative accomplishments ranged from divestment of state pension funds from businesses involved with South Africa to the creation of the nation's first state-wide Child Abuse Prevention Training Program and landmark affirmative action legislation guaranteeing women and minorities participation in the state's procurement opportunities.

While in the Assembly, Congresswoman Waters created the first opportunity for minorities and women to mange the state's vast public pension funds (some $100 billion in assets). She also successfully steered into law a bill to prevent strip searches for persons accused of non-violent misdemeanors and legislation to help prevent chemical catastrophes.

In Washington, Waters was a primary sponsor of a proposal to open up and reform the contracting process of the Resolution Trust Corporation (RTC) to include more minorities and women. She successfully worked to include minority and women contracting provisions in the committee's version of the Defense Production Act. She sponsored and passed an amendment in committee to extend legal services to veterans who are denied reemployment upon their return from military service.

She serves on the boards of directors of Essence Magazine, TransAfrica Foundation, the National Women's Political Caucus, the Center for National Policy, the Clara Elizabeth Jackson Carter Foundation (Spelman College), the National Minority AIDS Project and the National Commission for Economic Conversion and Disarmament.

A native of St. Louis, Missouri, Congresswoman Waters earned a Bachelor of Arts degree from California State University.

Maxine Waters

United States House of Representatives
35th Congressional District

Maxine Waters

[Speeches given to the House of Representatives.]

[May 14, 1992. This speech refers to the Los Angeles riots of 1992 which followed the verdict in the Rodney King case against the Los Angeles Police Department officers involved in his arrest.]

Mr. Speaker, I rise in support of H.R. 5132, the emergency supplemental appropriation for disaster assistance. This is the least that we can do to deal with the rebellion in Los Angeles and the flood situation in Chicago.

We are the United States of America, an interdependent system of government, and we certainly do take care of each other when disasters occur. That should not even be debatable. But let me just use this opportunity to say that this certainly is just a beginning. We respond to the emergency here at the moment, but there is much work to be done.

Our cities are in trouble in America. Our cities are in trouble because they have been neglected for far too long.

Mr. Speaker, we have thousands of young men and women who are unemployed, who live nowhere, sometimes with mother, sometimes with grandmother, sometimes under bridges. We have young men and women with no job training, many of whom have dropped out of school, even those who have graduated from high school who have no prospects of getting employed. We have exported jobs to Third World countries for cheap labor.

I live in South-Central Los Angeles. My district office was burned to the ground. My home is within one block of where the insurrection started. I know this community. I have watched in horror as it has been neglected in so many ways.

Not only did we export jobs, Mr. Speaker. Goodyear closed down. Bethlehem Steel closed down. Firestone closed down. This is where young people, even if they did not go to college, had reasonable expectations that they would get a job.

Today it is Los Angeles, but tomorrow it is anywhere in America. It is any city that could go up in flames. And let me say to those in suburbia, you do not exist in a vacuum. You are connected to the cities. Many of the services that you need are in the cities. Many of the jobs are in the cities.

We must live together in this nation in harmony. If we are to do it, we must recognize what has taken place, and we will move in a substantive way following this emergency assistance to deal with the real problems in the system, the root causes of what has taken place in Los Angeles. I am optimistic that we are going to do that.

I do not look at the president's six-point plan as the answer. I do not look at the package that the majors are bringing forth as the answer. I do not look at my own ideas as the answer. We have got to roll up our sleeves and get in the room together, both sides of the aisles, and we have got to decide what is good for America. When we put aside partisan, petty politics and do that kind of work, we will respond in ways that will help us to move forward in this country. I am delighted to be here to be part of this process.

Mr. Speaker, I look forward to what we are going to do.

. . .

[July 2, 1992, Debate on H.R. 11, Revenue Tax Bill.]

Mr. Speaker, I rise in support of this legislation. I support this legislation because the cities are in trouble. My own community is in trouble. We are desperate for help.

I support enterprise zones as an experiment. I am not sure that they will work. I know that I have worked on this bill to create some funding for social programs and not simply have an enterprise zone that would simply give tax credits to the corporations. We have covered in this legislation job training, we also have community policing, child-care investments and public housing, low-interest loan guarantees for cities. Is it enough? No, it is not. It is $2.5 billion. I think we need somewhere in the neighborhood of $30 billion to $40 billion to $50 billion to deal with the problems of the cities. Perhaps this is a beginning.

I want to say to the president of the United States of America he has got his enterprise zones. He has been able to give a whole lot of tax credits. We have created a new concept about what enterprise zones should be, by putting these social programs in here.

We need more money, we need more support. I have created a new program that will give stipends to young people from 17 to 30 who are in training, perhaps with support for the first time. Is it enough? No. Is it a beginning? Perhaps yes.

I am going to be watching this bill as it goes through the other body and when it comes back here with a conference report, to make sure that that money is in here for us to fund these programs. If it is not, I am not going to support a conference report.

. . .

[July 29, 1992]

Mr. Speaker, exactly three months ago today, the city of Los Angeles erupted in flames, frustration, and anger. We were told, "Be patient, help is on the way." We're still waiting, but our patience is wearing thin.

The $1.1 billion supplemental appropriations bill signed by the president replenished the FEMA [Federal Emergency Management Agency] and SBA [Small Business Administration] disaster accounts by $300 million—and spread $500 million for summer jobs programs across the country. That money has come and gone in six weeks.

The urban aid package passed by the House is only an experiment. Generous tax breaks on businesses and a pittance for job training and social programs. Maybe—a few years from now—they will result in new jobs in our communities. The Senate, the president's signature and an application process are yet to come.

We are on the brink of funding aid to Russia and a $10 billion loan guarantee for Israel. I certainly understand the difficulties faced by Russia—their economy has collapsed—and Israel—they must absorb tens of thousands of new immigrants. However, our cities deserve the same preference.

I have developed a $10 billion loan guarantee program for America's cities. It will be used for housing, small business, and economic development. I hope to see this plan adopted before we aid any foreign government. I request my colleagues' support for this endeavor. Our cities simmer with anticipation. Their hopes must not be dashed.

Kathleen Brown

A native Californian, Kathleen Brown might be said to have grown up with the state: both her father, Edmund G. "Pat" Brown, and her brother, Edmund G. "Jerry" Brown Jr., have served as governors of California. She is a lawyer, a graduate of Stanford University and Fordham University School of Law.

Before her election as state treasurer in 1990, Brown gained years of experience in public finance. As an elected member of the Board of Education for the Los Angeles Unified School District (in 1975 and again in 1979), she had responsibility for the second-largest school district in the country. Later she served as a corporate attorney specializing in public finance with the law firm of O'Melveny and Myers in New York and Los Angeles. In 1987, she was appointed to the Los Angeles Board of Public Works which oversees the city's sewers, streets, garbage, waste treatment facilities and other maintenance projects.

On January 7, 1991, Brown became California's 28th state treasurer, the second woman to hold the position. As treasurer, Brown is the state's official banker, involved in nearly every aspect of public finance. She is responsible for managing the state's $20 billion investment portfolio. She administers bond sales to finance schools, parks, prisons, housing, health facilities and environmental programs. She also serves as chair or a member of more than forty financing boards, authorities and commissions.

As a board member of the $67 billion California Public Employees' Retirement System (CalPERS)—the largest public pension fund in the nation—Brown introduced a motion passed by the board to ban junk bond investments. She has taken an active role in the fight against excessive executive pay both on the PERS board and as chair of the State Teachers' Retirement System subcommittee on corporate governance. She received much praise for her nonpartisan behavior during the heated budget crisis in the summer of 1992.

Brown is running for governor and faces a Democratic primary election in June, 1994.

Kathleen Brown

Treasurer

Kathleen Brown

[Speech given at New Visions Economic Conference, Bel Air Hotel, February 24, 1992.]

Today we've heard a lot of ideas about a new vision for California's economy.

It's long overdue.

Up in Sacramento, you don't hear much about vision; what you hear is that California is a "bad product."

And in the nation's magazines and newspapers, you don't read about our state's economic diversity and long-term vibrancy—you read about "doom and gloom."

The leader of that pack may well be my friend Bob Reinhold, who writes for the *New York Times* and who is with us here today.

If it's not our economy, Bob is writing about our devastating fires or our mudslides or our droughts.

That is why I was so relieved to recently read a story by Bob out of Las Vegas about the Nevada economy.

Finally, I thought, some bad news about somebody else!

I was so excited as I read the story I even thought about writing Bob a letter.

And then I got to the last paragraph, and do you know what it said?

"But Nevada's economic troubles are merely the result of the backdraft from the California recession."

I think it's time Bob and I sit down for a long talk.

Not that I would disagree with him about everything.

In fact, there is plenty to be gloomy about: budget shortfalls and a stubborn and severe national recession that has taken a very real toll on California workers, 8.1 percent of whom are unemployed—almost one in five of all jobless Americans.

California is losing more jobs per year than it's accustomed to creating each year.

And there is a tangible business malaise stemming from overregulation, high business costs, and the lack of meaningful workers' compensation insurance reform.

Then there's been the one-two-three punch "body blows" from the credit agencies, which have downgraded our credit to AA, AA1 and AA+.

All that is on top of the decade-old problems of high housing costs, overcrowded schools, gridlocked roads, and deteriorating and inadequate infrastructure.

But I believe these sights and sounds of crisis should be viewed instead as an *opportunity*...an opportunity to pick ourselves up and set ourselves right so we can move swiftly and smartly into what I believe can be the California century.

How do we get there?

First, we begin with a few basics:

As a first priority, we have got to put our fiscal house in order—moving the focus from the revenue side, where it was last year, to the expenditure side.

Next, government *must* get back to basics and consolidate, "downsize" and "right size" itself.

It's time, too, to reform and restructure government by restoring majority-vote passage of the budget in the legislature, adopting two-year budgets, and looking into changing the requirements for passing initiatives that deal with budget matters.

Next, we must preserve and invest in our infrastructure—both physical and intellectual.

To preserve our *intellectual infrastructure*, we need to invest in our educational systems, because smart, educated kids grow up to be smart and educated workers who can help us be more efficient and more competitive in a global economy.

At the same time, we need to rethink how we educate our kids.

They are as different as the world they live in: *it makes no sense to impose a 20th century education system on 21st century kids.*

What does make sense is a proposal to charter new public schools—an innovative step toward giving parents and teachers control over their kids' education.

It also makes sense to go back and take a fresh look at California's master plan for higher education, which was drawn up in 1960—long before the advent of fax machines, microwaves, VCR's, personal computers and satellite communication.

Next, we must invest in *physical infrastructure* because it creates an environment for economic development and it enhances environmental quality of life in a growing state.

The sad fact is, *we are not keeping up.*

Our last big build-and-invest era was in 1958-1966, when per-capita spending on infrastructure in constant dollars was $26 per person—*one-third higher* than the $17 per person that we've been spending over the last eight years.

The voters know it's important: they've voted for billions in bonds to build roads, transit systems and schools.

And *I* know it's important: as treasurer, I sold a record $4 billion last year and another $1.4 billion so far this year in the *largest* [state bond sale] in history at one of the *lowest interest rates* since Eisenhower crossed the Rhine.

But as important as *"how must we invest"* is *"what"* we invest in.

When we build, *we must build for the future!*

So when we talk about *new roads*, let's think instead about *smart highways*.

When we build new *school buildings*, let's design them for *computer-readiness* and *year-round utilization*.

And when we authorize new *rail systems*, let's make sure they're 'state of the art' like *bullet trains*—not trolleys from the last century.

Finally, let us seek to *reinvent government* so that it does not get left behind, unable to keep up with our new economy.

We need to *privatize* when appropriate, and encourage more *public/private partnerships*.

And we need to *reshape and refocus bureaucracies* created decades ago to *solve problems* that in many cases no longer exist.

Government today is too rule-ridden. It's like the two groundskeepers, one of whom spends the entire day digging holes while the other follows behind to fill them in. When asked by a passer-by what in the world they are doing, the reply is simple—and classic government-ese: "Because," says the digger, "the guy who puts the trees in the holes is out sick."

We lack flexibility, from the way we manage government workers to the way we do *budgets*.

It is reasonable to demand that government *leverage its resources* to make them go further and be used with greater efficiency.

Finally, government must change in another, more fundamental way: *it needs a top-to-bottom attitude adjustment*.

Government at all levels has forgotten its mission, *which is to serve*.

We have every right as taxpayers to be treated by government the same way businesses treat *their* customers.

Yet when was the last time you felt valued at your children's school or at the DMV, or at City Hall?

An entrepreneurial government which puts its customers first cannot help but be more efficient, more responsive and more innovative.

The key is in unbridling ourselves from *old rules, old regulations* and *old ways of thinking* that stand in the way of achieving the results that Californians *can* and *should* expect from their government.

We must, in short, reinvent government so that it can help, not hinder, California's march toward sustained economic prosperity.

To paraphrase the cartoon character Pogo's insightful observation—"I have met the enemy and it is us"—well, *I have met the future, and it is California*.

By the same token, the future of California should *not* be regarded as the enemy, but as an opportunity.

The shift from an *industrial and manufacturing-based economy* to a *service and information economy* plays to California's three greatest strengths—*trade, tourism and technology.*

These *"three T's"* add to our state's enviable economic diversity, and promise to provide continued opportunities for our wonderfully diverse and growing population.

There are also economic sectors that share one thing in common: they are in constant transition.

Ideas, products, and trends are born, mature and are replaced by new ideas, products, and trends.

They promise a never-ending cycle of change and growth in our increasingly global economic marketplace.

Yes, these *are* difficult times.

But we have seen difficult times before.

Our future is limited only by those leaders of narrow vision in both the public *and* private sectors who cannot see our future and therefore are afraid to invest in it.

A very wise California leader once said: "I have too much faith in California to accept the counsels of fear. With our people, energetic and prosperous, we provide a major market and a major reservoir of skilled employees...wise capital and good capital know this. They will come."

That very wise California leader was my father, who spoke those words one month into his administration *32 years ago*!

California faced an uncertain economic future then, as it does today.

But I, too, have faith: The 21st century can still be California's century.

Thank you.

Joyce Kennard

*J*oyce Kennard was born in Bandung, West Java, Indonesia, formerly the Dutch East Indies, of Dutch/Indonesian/Chinese ancestry. At age ten, she moved with her widowed mother from Java to Dutch New Guinea, now Irian Jaya. Four years later, she moved to Holland, and in 1961 immigrated alone to the United States where she became a naturalized citizen.

In 1971, she earned her B.A. degree, *magna cum laude*, from the University of Southern California while on academic scholarships and working at least 20 hours a week; she was elected a member of *Phi Beta Kappa*. In 1974, she earned a master's degree in public administration (receiving the Pfiffner Award for outstanding thesis of the academic year) and a law degree (receiving the American Jurisprudence Award in Torts) from the University of Southern California.

She began her legal career as a deputy attorney general in Los Angeles and later became a senior attorney in the state Court of Appeal in Los Angeles. In 1986, Governor George Deukmejian appointed her to the Municipal Court, and in 1987 he elevated her to the Superior Court in Los Angeles County. In 1988, she became an associate justice in the state Court of Appeal, Division Five, Los Angeles.

She has held her present position, associate justice of the California Supreme Court, since 1989 following nomination by Governor Deukmejian to replace Justice John Arguelles, who had retired. In November, 1990, the voters of California confirmed her to serve the remaining four years of her predecessor's term. Justice Kennard speaks for women and minorities, including, as an amputee herself, the physically disabled. A sample of the awards she has received:

"Outstanding Accomplishment as a Supreme Court Justice," 1991, the Asian/Pacific Women's Network, Los Angeles.

"Justice of the Year," 1991, the California Trial Lawyers Association.

"Chinese-American Pioneers from Southern California in the Judiciary" award, 1992, the Chinese Historical Society of Southern California.

Joyce Kennard

Associate Justice
California Supreme Court

Joyce L. Kennard

[Speech given at the Annual Meeting Program of the American Bar Association
Commission on Minorities at the Hilton Hotel,
San Francisco, August 8, 1992.]

*I*t gladdens my heart to see so many minority lawyers who know their proper place:
rubbing elbows with the good old boys at the ABA Convention.

Recently, Eva Paterson, an African-American civil rights attorney, wrote a fascinating
article for "California Lawyer," a publication of the California Bar. She observed that
"discourse about racism cannot be limited to African-American and white communities." She
points out that California's history in particular "has been shaped profoundly by Native
American, Asian-Pacific American and Latino communities that were restricted by law from
the state's earliest days."

Thus, in 1854 the California Supreme Court held in *People* v. *Hall* that "Chinese and
other people not white" could not testify against a white person. Congress passed laws
excluding the Chinese and the Japanese from immigration into this country. There was an
immigration quota for Filipinos, whose annual quota was restricted to 50. Filipinos were
considered to be savages, but then so were African-Americans and the Chinese. Mexican-
American children were segregated in the public schools not because of race—they were
considered white—but because of language problems and personal hygiene. Asian Indians too
were considered Caucasian but unclean.

As I started delving into books and articles in preparing for this speech, I noticed that
whatever traits were associated with a particular minority would in time be associated with
other minorities. Minorities in general were considered to be inferior, savage, heathen, dirty,
and lustful.

Undoubtedly it was concern for the danger that these lustful minorities posed to the
purity of the white race that led to the enactment of anti-miscegenation laws. In his book,
Strangers from a Different Shore, A History of Asian Americans (1989), Professor Ronald Takaki
mentions that as early as 1661, Maryland had enacted a law prohibiting marriage between
whites and blacks. By the 19th century, such laws existed in most states. California, in 1880,
enacted legislation specifically prohibiting marriage between a white person and "a negro,
mulatto, or mongolian." Only two years earlier, at the 1878 California Constitutional
Convention, John F. Miller warned: "Were the Chinese to amalgamate at all with our people,
it would be the lowest, most vile and degraded of our race, and the result of that

amalgamation would be a hybrid of the most despicable, a mongrel of the most detestable that has ever afflicted the earth" (p. 101). I am such a mongrel.

I was born in 1941 in West Java, Indonesia, then part of the Dutch Colonial Empire. My parents came from a mixed heritage: Chinese, Indonesian, and European. My father died in a Japanese internment camp before I was one year old. Until the liberation of the islands by the allied troops in 1945, I spent my early years in an internment camp, together with my mother and my Chinese grandmother.

After Indonesia gained its independence from the Dutch in 1949, my mother and I moved to West New Guinea, at that time mostly impenetrable jungle and the last remaining colony of the Dutch. My mother worked as a typist for a Dutch oil company in a small town largely controlled by the oil company. The company had segregated living areas for its employees.

Employees hired in Holland lived in areas separate from those hired in Indonesia. It does not take long to figure out that those hired in Holland were Dutch, whereas the other hirees were either Indonesian or mixed Indonesian/Dutch.

My mother and I lived in a non-white area in a quonset hut, which we shared with four families. Our bathroom was an outside enclosure that contained an oil drum filled with water. One would simply dip an empty can into the water and pour it over the body. The toilet was a cement ditch far from the hut, on the edge of the jungle.

The white school was off limits. I attended a tiny missionary school with children whose ancestors had only recently stepped out of the stone age and given up the practice of cannibalism. Also off limits was the big Dutch store; my mother and I bought our necessities from the Chinese storekeeper, such as a thermos of ice cubes at noon every day so we could have some ice water to get some relief from the blistering heat. Once in a while we were able to buy fresh fish from native peddlers: the women were bare-breasted and the men wore only a loincloth. Otherwise we would rely on dried salted fish or a can of corned beef to add to our staple of steamed rice.

As a ten-year-old child growing up in the inhospitable jungles of New Guinea, I did not know that I was being discriminated against. To me, it was simply a fact of life that I lived in a non-white area, went to a non-white school, and was not allowed in the white store.

That is my frame of reference with respect to racial discrimination, a childhood experience in a country other than America. The incident that I will next describe involved racial discrimination in America against an African-American, Justice Edwin Jefferson, who retired from the State Court of Appeal in Los Angeles in 1975.

Justice Edwin Jefferson, the brother of retired Justice Bernard Jefferson, was admitted to the California Bar in 1931, appointed to the Municipal Court in 1941 by Governor Culbert

Olsen, elevated to the Superior Court in 1948 by Governor Earl Warren, and elevated to the state Court of Appeal in 1961 by Governor Edmund Brown.

The incident I am about to describe was related by Justice Edwin Jefferson to his research attorney, who is a friend of mine. She in turn related the story to me.

When Edwin Jefferson was elevated (either to the Superior Court or the Court of Appeal—I'm not sure), the governor had a formal dinner for him at the exclusive Jonathan Club in Los Angeles, traditionally a club where only white males of a certain background could become members.

On the night of the dinner in his honor, Edwin Jefferson arrived at the main entrance of the club. As he prepared to enter, he was told that blacks were not welcome. He explained that he was the guest of honor at a dinner hosted by the governor. He still could not get in. So he headed towards the service entrance.

He went into the kitchen and told the waiters, who were black, about what had just transpired. He then borrowed a linen towel from the headwaiter, put it over his arm, took a tray with glasses, and walked up to the governor, to whom he said: "I'm your appointee. This is the only way I could get in to attend the banquet you're having in my honor." The governor was shocked.

Undoubtedly you have your own personal story of discrimination because you happened to be black, white, yellow, brown, or in-between. All of us, either personally or through our forebears, came as strangers from many a different shore. Some came voluntarily, others involuntarily.

As Professor Takaki has observed, the distinguishing physical features of minorities became their "racial uniforms." Until recently, the prevailing vision was that America was "essentially a place where European immigrants would establish a homogeneous white society and where non-whites would have to remain 'strangers'" (*Strangers*, p. 472).

We have come a long way from the bad old days, when minorities were relegated to the bottom rungs of the career ladder. Although acceptance and advancement have been very slow in coming, the important thing is that today we are penetrating the bastions of power. Our presence here today is proof of that. The goal is to get more minorities into the bastions of power. For minority lawyers, that means access to membership in the judiciary.

When Diane Yu invited me to speak here, she asked that I discuss the "pitfalls and frustrations" that minority judges face.

To be asked to speak to a group of minorities can in itself be a pitfall, at least in my case. I am a mixture of various disfavored groups. I am a woman, I am multi-racial, I am an above-the-knee-amputee, and I am an immigrant, with an accent. The accent immediately identifies me as a stranger from another shore.

Because there are so few minorities in positions of authority, those of us who happen to occupy such a position and who fit into more than one "disfavored group" category bear the added burden of having to speak for broad classes of people, with each class having its own distinct interest at heart.

With respect to Diane's request that I talk about the frustrations minority judges face, presumably Diane used the term minority judge to refer to racial or ethnic background rather than a judge who is almost always in the court's minority in the decision-making process. You see, as a frequent dissenter on the seven-member California Supreme Court, I fit that minority label too.

Being a judge of a particular racial or ethnic minority is difficult. One has to battle against stereotyping. When one is a woman to boot, there is double difficulty. For thousands of years, women have been told that they are the inferior sex.

As a judge who happens to be a woman with a multi-racial background, the frustration comes to some extent from being classified and misclassified by various publications and individuals trying to make various points. I have been classified as Asian, as white, as Eurasian, and as Chinese. Once, a publication referred to me as a "white male."

The very fact that I, a woman judge of mixed racial heritage, am subject to this arbitrary classification process shows that women and minorities are woefully underrepresented in the judiciary. If the composition of the bench roughly represented the composition of society as a whole, all this effort in classification would be both uninteresting and pointless.

In short, for me, a woman and a racial minority, the obvious frustration is that there are too few of us on the bench.

In recent years, America's population has rapidly become multi-racial, multi-ethnic, and multi-cultural. That diversity should be reflected in the judiciary. Fair access to the courts means more than ensuring a litigant his or her day in court; it also means access to jurists who reflect a cross-section of society.

Do minority judges make a difference? The general response given by people is: "Yes, they do. The diversity in background that judges from various racial or ethnic groups bring to the bench may result in a diversity of views and perspectives that would add to, rather than diminish, the fairness of the decision-making process." Intrigued by the response, I quickly reviewed in my mind some of my decisions. I'll briefly touch on one of them.

That case involved a 55-year-old African American male, Robert Cannon, a retired electrician who, because of his race, had been denied the right to rent an apartment at a 418-unit complex for people 55 years old and over. He was put on a waiting list for 2½ years. Only through pure happenstance did Cannon find out that whites had no problem renting an apartment.

Cannon filed a complaint with the state [Fair Empoyment and] Housing Commission, which awarded him damages that included $50,000 for emotional distress and $35,000 in punitive damages. A majority of the seven-member California Supreme Court struck down most of that award, allowing Cannon only $2,800 for his actual out-of-pocket expenses and $1,000 in punitive damages. By the way, at the time of our decision Cannon was 67 years old.

The majority held that the commission did not have the power to award damages for emotional distress and humiliation resulting from discrimination because such damages were in the majority's view "not reasonably necessary" to accomplish the commission's statutory goal of preventing and redressing discrimination.

I dissented. I pointed out that the purpose of the statutory scheme was to prevent and redress discrimination in housing. Such discrimination cannot be adequately redressed when its victims are denied compensation for the real and grievous injuries of humiliation and distress. Thus I would have upheld the commission's award of $50,000 for the emotional distress Cannon had suffered. And, unlike the majority, I would have upheld the $35,000 in punitive damages as a deterrent.

Only one justice joined my dissent. That was Allen Broussard, the only other minority on the seven-member Court. Did Allen and I bring a certain sensitivity or understanding to this particular case because of our background? You be the judge.

Whatever life experience a particular minority member may bring to the bench, the important thing to remember is that in the long run respect for and confidence in the judiciary will be achieved only if the public perceives that our system of justice is presided over by a judiciary that is not monochromatic but reflects the diversity of the larger society itself. That's what fairness means: having the fate of litigants of various hues and colors decided by a judiciary of various hues and colors.

I realize that as long as people come in various hues and colors, there will be prejudice. It is a fact of life that is common not only to America, but also to the rest of the world. Does that mean that we should accept discrimination? Never.

Yes, we have problems in America, and minorities bear the scars to prove the wounds that were inflicted on them in the struggle for equality. But, to borrow a phrase from Martin Luther King Jr. let us not seek to satisfy our thirst for justice "by drinking from the cup of bitterness and hatred. We must forever conduct our struggle on the high plane of dignity and discipline."

America still is the land of opportunity, liberty, and hope. America is still striving to become what no other country in the world has ever been: a nation of many races and ethnic groups trying to exist peacefully side by side. Perhaps one day, instead of being a hyphenated American, we can simply be American, with pride in our racial and ethnic heritage. Only then will we see the realization of the dream Martin Luther King Jr. had: that one day this nation will not judge its residents by the color of their skin but by the content of their character. Only then will America truly be a great nation.

We minority judges would not be where we are today without the support of groups such as this. You made our success possible. And now we need to make room for you, the new judges of this nation.

If you want to become a judge, and you possess the requisite qualifications, do not wait to be asked. Apply. Above all, persevere. You have much to gain, and so does America. As equal participants in the judiciary, you will help make the administration of justice more representative of the rich mosaic that is America, which is, by birth or by choice, your land and my land.

Alice Lytle

$\mathscr{B}$orn in Jersey City, New Jersey, Alice Lytle was raised in New York City from the age of five. She graduated from Hunter College with a degree in psychology and public health. She worked as a medical research technician at the Albert Einstein College of Medicine of Yeshiva University, where she had charge of an animal research laboratory for the pediatric cardiologist, Dr. Abraham Rudolph. She later decided on a career in law and graduated from Hastings College of Law in San Francisco. At Hastings, she was president of the Black Law Students Association and worked as a law clerk for the National Association for the Advancement of Colored People (NAACP) and attorneys in private practice, gaining a reputation for her balanced "judicial" temperament.

She began her legal career as an assistant in a public defender's office, then moved to research in rural housing administration and teaching criminal law. Governor Edmund G. "Jerry" Brown Jr. appointed her his deputy legal affairs secretary in charge of extradition and executive clemency matters, and other legal assignments. He appointed her to two other positions: chief of the state Division of Fair Employment Practices and then secretary of the State and Consumer Services Agency, a Cabinet-level post. Her responsibilities included general management of over thirteen departments and programs such as the Francise Tax Board, the Department of Fair Employment and Housing, the Department of Consumer Affairs, the Office of State Fire Marshal, the Department of General Services, the Public Employees' Retirement System, the State Personnel Board, the Department of Veterans Affairs, the California Museum of Science and Industry and the California Public Broadcasting Commission.

In January, 1983, Governor Brown appointed her to the Sacramento Municipal Court. She has been re-elected and served as presiding judge with administrative authority over 300 court employees and over twenty judicial positions. Always an advocate for children, she created "La Casita" a children's waiting room. She works for children as a volunteer in a "godparent" program and teaches "high-risk" third-to-ninth graders through the Black Sacramento Christian Club.

In 1980, she was admitted to the Hunter College Hall of Fame; in 1983, she received the YWCA "Woman of the Year" award in law, and in 1990, the "Jurist of the Year" award from the San Francisco Women Lawyers Alliance.

Alice Lytle

Judge, Juvenile Division
Superior Court of the State of California
County of Sacramento

Alice Lytle

[We received this letter with Judge Alice Lytle's speech:

September 15, 1992

Pursuant to your request I am sending the enclosed speech. Though short and made to a very small audience, I consider this speech to be among the most significant I have made in my life.

The speech was made to a man sent to my department in the Municipal Court for jury trial on a charge of spousal abuse. He was African-American, an ex-FBI agent, in his early 40s and the father of six children. The family was obviously suffering under immense pressure and although I could not, under the circumstances, learn all the family dynamics I could see that a jury trial with its attendant tension and conflict was the last thing this family needed. The deputy district attorney and the assistant public defender were both convinced that the defendant should be diverted. Diversion involves counseling of the family and, if successfully completed, results in the dismissal of all charges. However, the defendant was adamant that his wife's behavior had "provoked" him and he was therefore innocent and refused diversion, insisting on his trial and further insisting that as the children had been witnesses to the alleged assault he would call them as witnesses against their mother.

I wrote and made the enclosed speech and asked the gentleman to go home and think it over. He did and the next day (after the jury had been called) he agreed to diversion. Of all the speeches I have made this one without a doubt had the most significant consequences.]

We workers within the criminal justice system are enamored of labels. These labels serve a purpose. They help us categorize and arrange exceedingly complex situations. In a very real sense, however, they are very unhelpful. Indeed they can be counterproductive. These labels can conceal and confuse a multitude of emotional and psychological dynamics. They can also feed pre-existing feelings of anger and helplessness. The label "defendant" may have started out life as a relatively innocuous word, but its use within the criminal justice context now carries some alarmingly negative connotations. The word "victim" as used within the criminal justice setting doesn't begin to encompass the number and variety of persons who come within the definition. Many a defendant has come before the bar of justice feeling every bit as victimized as the prosecuting witness and many a victim comes into court feeling no small amount of fault for the situation that led to the criminal charges.

The criminal process is a blame-seeking mechanism. In any given situation such as this one can find, depending on one's point of view, plenty of blame to go around. A jury may find a defendant in the spousal abuse case not guilty. The defendant's sense of vindication must, however, be tempered by the acknowledgement of some very grim facts. First, a finding of not guilty is not the same as a finding of innocence. It simply means that the prosecution could not provide the jury with sufficient evidence to enable a jury to find proof of guilt beyond a reasonable doubt—a very high standard of proof. It sounds like the most egregious kind of hairsplitting, but it makes a difference to a defendant such as yourself who feels wronged. Secondly, a finding of not guilty, if it comes, only comes after the trauma and stress of a criminal trial which will expose all the very personal matters of you and your family to strangers. Ordinarily a man such as yourself would vigorously guard his family against such an outrageous invasion of privacy. If the verdict is guilty, then in addition to the stress of the trial, you will be faced with the prospect, at the worst, of a jail sentence and at the very least a criminal conviction record.

You feel strongly that the defendant in this matter should be your wife and not yourself. I cannot comment on that except to say this—what difference does it make to your children whether it is their father or their mother facing criminal prosecution? If one of them is, God forbid, placed on the witness stand to testify, what possible difference will it make to that child that he or she is testifying against his mother instead of his father? Will the pain for that child be any less?

You are obviously a man of substance. I have not met your wife, but I must assume that she is a woman of substance. I must believe that you both have the intellectual and emotional resources to repair this tear in the fabric of your family. But you need help in doing it. You will not find that help within the setting of a criminal trial. You will find it if you allow this case to be taken out of the criminal justice system and placed where it belongs—within the hands of professional family counselors. This diversion process will neither require nor imply an admission of guilt. Unlike the jury trial process it will not expose you and your family to public view. To ensure success it will require the cooperation and commitment of all members of the family. Within the counseling setting no one will be defendant and no one will be victim. Bear in mind that you give up very little if you decide on diversion. That is, if the diversion is unsuccessful, you still have your right to a jury trial. You will have to give up your right to a speedy trial since your trial will be delayed pending the results of counseling.

Too often in this court I have seen people who are wounded and hurt seeking to use the criminal justice system to strike out at a perceived wrongdoer. Most times this is appropriate behavior, particularly when the perceived wrongdoer is a stranger and the wrong clear and unambiguous. This is not such a case. It is possible that you may secure what you feel is a victory in this case. Such a victory will be a hollow one and the war will go on. Included among the casualties will be your children.

Marian Bergeson

A former teacher, school board member and president of the California School Boards Association, Marian Bergeson is serving her third term as a state senator. She represented Southern California as an Assembly member from 1978 to 1984 and as a senator from 1984 to the present. Her 35th Senate District includes all of Orange County.

Bergeson chairs the Senate Local Government Committee, one of only three Republicans in the Legislature to supervise a standing policy committee. Her efforts to bring fiscal responsibility and sensible growth planning to California's cities and counties are well respected. She also serves as a member of the committees on Appropriations, Ethnics, Health and Human Services, Industrial Relations, Transportation, and serves as vice chair of Housing and Urban Affairs.

In 1990, the California Journal named her the top Republican senator for her honesty, intelligence, energy and effectiveness. She describes her most significant legislative achievements as her bills that brought prenatal health care to California's low-income women and children, reduced personal tax burdens by preventing automatic income-tax increases, and which carefully integrated private-sector efficiency into the state Department of Transportation.

Bergeson describes her most significant legislative achievements relating to education as her bills that reformed the teacher credentialling process, authorized critical bond funds for school facilities, and provided for higher curriculum standards and graduation requirements.

A 30-year resident of Newport Beach, she is running for the Orange County Board of Supervisors in the June, 1994, election.

Marian Bergeson

California State Senate
35th Senatorial District

Marian Bergeson

["Redevelopment Agencies: The New Cash Cows in California," speech given to California Public Finance Conference, San Francisco Hyatt Regency, September 17, 1992.]

*R*edevelopment has literally changed the way that California looks!

The downtowns in San Francisco, Los Angeles, Santa Ana, Sacramento, and San Jose exist because of redevelopment. Tens of thousands of low-income families live in better conditions. Redevelopment officials created 23,000 new jobs in 1990 and built 20 million square feet in new construction.

For many California communities, redevelopment primes the pump for economic development and job retention. So why all the fuss?

An old axiom tells us that "success has many parents but failure is always an orphan." Well, in redevelopment's case, there's a real extended family!

One of redevelopment's most indulgent parents is the state general fund. At least 35 cents of every tax increment dollar is an indirect subsidy from the state general fund. According to the legislative analyst's office, redevelopment cost the state general fund as much as $400 million in 1989; three years later, the price tag is even higher.

In 1990-91, redevelopment agencies generated about $1.2 billion in property tax increment revenues! Even in a huge state like California, those are indeed adult dollars!

Think about it: redevelopment is the state government's biggest economic development program. It dwarfs our spending on enterprise zones. It's bigger than disaster relief. It's much larger than the Deukmejian administration's old Rural Renaissance program.

Costing nearly a half-billion dollars a year, the state's subsidy to redevelopment projects is beyond the control of Governor Wilson and the California Legislature. The appropriation for redevelopment does not appear as a line-item in the annual state budget. State bureaucrats do not review redevelopment plans. Legislative committees do not control who gets the money or how local officials spend it!

All state law asks in return is relatively minor: set-aside 20 percent of the tax increment income from affordable housing. And even then, we don't see much performance.

Last December, my Senate Local Government Committee held an oversight hearing on redevelopment agencies' housing programs. We found that redevelopment officials had stockpiled about $700 million in housing set-aside funds.

Now, some redevelopment agencies have terrific records: San Jose and Sacramento have much to be proud of.

But then there's Culver City, sitting on $10 million in affordable housing money. We learned that Culver City produced exactly 18 dwelling units with its redevelopment funds in the last three years. That's a poor record by any measure. Failure may be an orphan, but in this case, we don't need a paternity test!

We should be using that set-aside money. We should be spending that money to build apartments for moderate-income people. We should be using that money to build houses for families buying their first homes. We should be using that money to put suppliers and builders back in business. We should be using that money to get carpenters, plumbers, electricians, and roofers back to work.

Local officials control those dollars; they can stimulate the local economy with a little pump priming of their own. They don't need to wait for permission from Sacramento.

My hearing stirred up local officials on this issue. The good redevelopment agencies were proud to stand up and explain their records. And I applauded. The others looked pretty nervous when we began to pressure them about affordable housing.

If local officials respond by spending the $700 million in set-aside money for affordable housing, then I will claim some maternal pride. Sometimes, a little firm encouragement is enough to prompt better behavior.

Speaking of better behavior, let me tell you about a redevelopment practice that is about to end. For good.

Some of you know it as the so-called "Coronado Plan." The redevelopment agency and the local school district team up to siphon millions of dollars out of the state general fund without any accountability.

The arrangement works like this. The city council declares the entire city to be "blighted." By the way, have you been to Coronado lately? That charming town between the blue Pacific and the lovely San Diego Bay sure didn't look very "blighted" to me...

Then the redevelopment agency redefines the property tax increment revenue so that the county government doesn't lose any revenue, the special districts don't lose anything, and even the city escapes the hit. Who's left? You guessed it: just the school district. Which means the state general fund!

The next step is for the redevelopment agency to skim off the increment but then turn around and build schools with it. This means that the state general fund must back-fill the school district for the money that the redevelopment agency will use to build schools for the school district.

In effect, the "Coronado Plan" is a clever money-laundering scheme that raids the state general fund to pay for school construction.

When this practice started spreading around Southern California, I began to get worried calls from my constituents. In the Riverside County hamlet of Hemet, city and school officials enthusiastically embraced the "Coronado Plan" as a way of building the schools they need.

Now, as a member of the Allocation Board [California's funding mechanism for public K-12 school facilities], I understand the very real need to build schools in our growing communities. After all, I've successfully authored nearly a billion dollars in statewide school construction bonds. But this is just not the proper way!

When I learned about Hemet's attempt, I contracted the director of the state Department of Finance. Tom [Hayes] and his staff quickly understood the connection between Hemet's intentions and the cost to the state general fund. At Tom's request, Attorney General Dan Lungren walked into court and filed against Hemet.

Confronted by court opposition from the California attorney general as well as local litigants, and faced with a voters' referendum, Hemet officials showed good judgment and stepped back from the "Coronado Plan."

The Hemet story marks a significant turning point in the fiscal relationship between redevelopment agencies and the state government.

For the first time, the Department of Finance saw the threat to the state general fund. For the first time, the attorney general challenged a redevelopment project. For the first time, local officials blinked and backed away.

State officials learned three important lessons from our Hemet experience:

First, we need to speak clearly to local officials about our unwillingness to subsidize school construction by the "Coronado Plan."

Second, we need better state oversight when redevelopment officials use state money. My own Senate Bill 1711 gives the Department of Finance standing to challenge redevelopment plans and amendments. It's not much of a watchdog, but it's better than what we've had.

Third, we need to change the law. Senate Bill 617, one of the budget trailer bills, declares that the absence of schools is not a sufficient justification for redevelopment. I expect Governor Wilson to sign SB 617.

In closing, I want to mention one other issue where redevelopment agencies are connected to the state general fund. To implement the state budget, we had to shift $1.3 billion from local governments to schools. This cut was very painful for those of us who support home rule and local control. But we had to do it.

Redevelopment's share is $200 million in 1992-93. That's about a 15 percent shift in property tax increment revenues from redevelopment agencies to local schools. While cities, counties, and special districts will suffer permanent cuts in property tax revenues, that hit on redevelopment agencies is just for the current fiscal year.

Is it too large? Of course it is! Just as the reduction is too large for every other type of local government.

But let me explain what might have happened. When the Senate drafted our own version of the local government package, we suggested a $120 million cut for redevelopment agencies. But we wanted to cut $120 million in both in the current fiscal year and in 1993-94. We also proposed a 2 1/2 year moratorium on new redevelopment projects and on major amendments to existing projects.

The Assembly responded with Assembly Bill 844, which we eventually passed and sent to Governor Wilson. There is no moratorium in AB 844 and the cut is just for one fiscal year. We expect the governor to sign that bill shortly.

So, is redevelopment a cash cow? Not really. I applaud the many successes of redevelopment, but caution you against letting the cow stray out of her proper pasture. For those of you directly involved in redevelopment, I caution you, too, to plan your projects wisely—redevelopment has developed its share of enemies over the past 30 years.

Redevelopment is both a boon and a boondoggle—and too many people would like to see it stumble.

Lucy Killea

*L*ucy Killea is a former Texan who came to California already experienced in national and international affairs. After graduation from Incarnate Word College in San Antonio, she worked in Washington as an information analyst for the United States Army Intelligence. In the post-war period, she went overseas with the United States delegation as an assistant to Eleanor Roosevelt at the United Nation's first General Assembly. Later she joined the CIA in Washington and became one of the highest-ranking women in American intelligence work.

In California, she and her husband settled in San Diego County. They have two grown sons. She studied at the University of San Diego for a master's degree in history and then earned a Ph.D. in Latin American history at the University of California, San Diego.

In 1978, her public service began with an appointment to the San Diego City Council. The following year she won election to the council with 71 percent of the vote. Her popularity continued as she served four terms in the California State Assembly. Her principal issues were crime prevention, bond finance, waste management and transportation.

In 1989, she was elected to the state Senate as a Democrat. In August, 1991, Killea ended her affiliation with the Democratic Party and re-registered as a nonpartisan. (She was re-elected in 1992 as an Independent). She is the only woman in the United States elected to partisan office as an Independent. She represents the 39th Senatorial District in San Diego.

Killea has developed policy expertise in the areas of bond finance, waste management, and transportation, as well as a broad spectrum of issues relating to the environment, women's health, education, law enforcement and political reform. She is the Senate appointee to the California Debt Advisory Commission and the Little Hoover Commission and chairs the Senate Commission on Corporate Governance.

Killea's hallmark has been a fearless, small "d" democratic faith in nonpartisan public service. She gives her reasons for disavowing party affiliation in the following speech, her "Declaration of Independence."

Lucy Killea

California State Senate
39th Senatorial District

Lucy Killea

[Speech given to the state Senate, Sacramento, California, August 19, 1991.]

*M*r. President and Members of the Senate:

During the summer recess all of us were able to return to our districts and listen to our constituents, hearing what they think about the job we're doing.

Now, setting aside our own individual job performances for a moment, what I'm hearing isn't good. This institution—the Senate, the Assembly, the Legislature as a whole—is in serious trouble. And I'm not talking about the budget and the difficult pills we have asked everyone to swallow—the tax increases or the cuts, or the dissatisfaction of chronic malcontents. I'm talking about a much deeper dissatisfaction, even resentment—a sense among a broad section of the public, without regard to political affiliation—that this Legislature is interested only in ITSELF.

No matter how noble our innermost motivations are, no matter how solid our records individually, the fact is that time after time we give the public very good reason to think that our first priority is to make sure we get our full per diem—that our first priority is to carve out districts favorable to our own ambition—that our first priority is to maintain a hefty balance in our campaign treasury to discourage a challenger.

This is what the public believes and I don't blame them. Oh, we can blame the press. We can blame negative political campaigns. We can blame initiatives. We can blame one special interest or another. We can even blame the other house or the other party or the governor. But ultimately, the responsibility is ours and ours alone.

Take for example something as small as the meals brought in during session. We have put Senator Roberti in a terribly awkward position of having to defend us. Listen to this excerpt from David Roberti's suggested response letter to a constituent concerned about the dinner brought into the Senate on July 14.

"Providing food is a prudent way of helping ensure that as many Members as possible are present."

Is this the best we can say for ourselves? I don't blame David Roberti for this. This is our collective responsibility. The same goes for the midnight Extraordinary Session where we conducted no business and collected four days of per diem on the Fourth of July weekend. It's simply not defensible. I've joined Senator Thompson in returning the per diem for that weekend.

We've lost the public's confidence. And if you doubt it, just ask them. Simply ask the question: Do you approve of the job the state Legislature is doing? You know the answer. If you don't trust public opinion polls, let's put it on the ballot. I would be surprised if we got 30 percent approving of our job. That's an "F" grade. And, ultimately we must face the music.

The answer is we must change—and change something more than district boundary lines. Reapportionment won't save this house. I fear it will only make things worse.

The answer is not to hide from the public behind gerrymandered lines of self-protection. Morally it is wrong. And practically, there simply aren't enough hiding places. We have lost the public's confidence, and it has been a failure of both political parties not to provide the leadership to regain it.

So, after more than 40 years as a registered Democrat I have decided to ask for your help to leave the Democratic Party and re-register as an Independent. I want to run for re-election in 1992.

I have a technical problem I need your assistance to resolve. You see, I can't leave the Democratic Party and seek re-election without your permission. That's right, the law simply doesn't allow it. In 1969, a law was written that prohibits anyone from seeking partisan office if they have changed party affiliation within 12 months prior to the *primary* election for the office sought. This means that anyone who changes their party registration, *in any way*, after June 2 of this year is ineligible to run for the Legislature in 1992. I was not aware of this until last week, when I had intended to re-register before returning to Sacramento.

This provision is an obvious attempt to limit the rights of individuals exercising their free choice in selecting party affiliation. I believe this statute is unconstitutional in that it places an additional eligibility requirement on prospective candidates beyond those specified in Article 4 Section 2 of the California Constitution. I have drafted amendments to the Independent nomination statute which would change the one-year period to 88 days, coinciding with the deadline for filing nomination papers in the party primary. This would allow not only me, but anyone else, the option of leaving their party and pursuing an Independent nomination without forfeiting our right to seek election. Incidentally, Independent nomination requires the substantial burden of obtaining signatures from 3 percent of the registered voters in one's district—in my case well over 10,000 signatures compared to the 50 required for partisan nomination. I will be asking for your support for this legislation when it comes before you in the days ahead.

While my change of party is for the most part symbolic, symbolic of my dissatisfaction with the ability of the party leadership to come to grips with the issue of political reform, it was still for me personally a very difficult decision to make, and I wanted to let you know why leaving the Democratic Party is not easy for me.

And if you'll allow me several more minutes, I'd like to tell you about the Democratic Party I joined and the one I want to leave.

I first registered to vote when I turned 21 in the summer following my final year at a Catholic college in San Antonio, Texas. I was signing up for the opportunity to vote for Franklin Delano Roosevelt whose name was on the ballot, and whose wife, Eleanor Roosevelt, I greatly admired.

The Roosevelts stood for the working men and women and for making sure that Americans had jobs, a roof over their heads and didn't go hungry. They stood for protecting women and children from abusive labor practices and for guaranteeing the security of retiring workers. And, in 1944, they stood more than anything for defending abroad the principles of freedom and democracy and defeating fascism.

I didn't just sign up to *vote* for the Roosevelts, I signed up to *work* for them. I went to Washington D.C. and found a place in military intelligence, and later, when the Central Intelligence Agency was formed, I worked there as well.

After World War II, I had the privilege of working with Eleanor Roosevelt herself. I was one of a number who went with her to London on the Queen Mary to the first meeting of the United Nations General Assembly.

It's difficult to say at what exact moment we are bitten by the bug of public service. In my case it was sometime on this trip when I, just 22 years old, saw Eleanor Roosevelt speaking to ambassadors from all over the world, all of them men, showing me that it was possible for a woman, even in the men's world of that time, to make a tremendous contribution to her country and the world. When it comes to role models you don't need many, you just need good ones.

In 1948 I missed my only election. I was in the Netherlands working on the reconstruction of Europe, the Marshall Plan, when Truman was elected without the benefit of my absentee ballot. I was so scared to death that Dewey had won that I haven't missed an election since.

My first involvement in electoral politics began in San Diego in the '70s, and I was always a nonpartisan participant. In fact, I really owe my appointment to the City Council more to Larry Stirling and Pete Wilson than I do the San Diego Democratic Party establishment. We managed to accomplish quite a bit in a nonpartisan fashion.

Then I moved into the Assembly where I had to wear a team jersey, Democrats on this side, Republicans on the other. It wasn't really my style but I played the game because that, I was told, was the only way it could be played. My district was equally divided between Democrats and Republicans and I always counted on support from both sides.

Then of course in 1989 I sought and won election to the Senate in what was described as a "safe Republican district." I ran as I always have, as someone who sought to offer a choice on issues instead of party loyalty. Over the past five years, in three very contentious elections, my constituents have indicated their support for my individual, non-partisan approach.

Last year, when I was new to this house, I announced with Common Cause that I supported Proposition 131, which would have established term limits of 12 years for all legislative offices, campaign spending reforms, and establishment of an independent prosecutor for political crimes—similar to legislation I had carried when in the Assembly. I know that term limits were no panacea of political reform, but this measure, with the campaign reforms I had supported in the past, provided a more intelligent response to what the public was rightfully demanding—major political reform.

My position was regarded as an act of heresy within my caucus and I was rebuked accordingly. The far more draconian measure, Proposition 140, passed, and the Legislature has suffered not only from the cuts, but from the spectacle of going to court to undo the public's will as expressed at the polls.

If successful, this lawsuit will do more damage to the Legislature as an institution than the measure itself. Imagine the outrage of the public when they learn that their effort to reform the Legislature, however clumsy it may have been, is tossed out by the court at the behest of the Legislature, and that the Legislature has offered no alternative in its stead except business as usual. Members, the cartographers cannot save us from this wrath, I promise you.

But I know this institution well enough to know that what I say on this subject will not alter the course chosen in pursuit of redistricting.

At least my announcement today should make the job easier. Do with my district what you will, without regard to party affiliation. I'm comfortable representing Democrats or Republicans or Independents in any configuration anywhere in San Diego County. In my mind, no district is safe or ought to be. Think about the phrase "safe district." Safe from what? Safe from whom? The voters? The notion of a safe district is an insult to the system of democracy.

My change in party doesn't indicate any change in my values, my philosophy, my legislative agenda, or my votes, nor any change in my commitment to work on these issues which I believe are more important to my constituents than anyone's party affiliation. Partisan Republicans should take little comfort in my move. Joining the Republican Party was never a consideration when I decided to leave this one.

As for your Californians who see no use in getting involved, I would still urge them more than ever to register to vote, to join a party if they so desire, but more importantly, to work for change. For me, I have come to conclude that I need to do something to get the message through to my colleagues and friends that things are indeed not well. This is my way of sounding an alarm.

For now, I have withheld from re-registering, but my intentions are unequivocal to do so after the law is changed. I have fought for choice all my life. Now, I would like to have a choice. And I would like the voters to have one as well.

In the meantime, I will continue as I have in the business of the house, but I will respectfully be excusing myself from meetings of the Democratic Caucus.

It's a difficult day for me, yet now, having said what I have felt needed saying for quite some time, I feel a burden has been lifted. I sincerely hope some good will come of it.

Thank you.

Diane E. Watson

A native Californian, Senator Watson is a lifetime resident of the senatorial district which she represents in the state Legislature. The district includes the communities of Venice, Marina Del Rey, Westchester, the Los Angeles International Airport, Crenshaw and Hancock Park. She graduated from the University of California, Los Angeles, and earned a master's degree in school psychology at California State University, Los Angeles. She attended the Kennedy School of Government at Harvard University in 1982 and finished a Ph.D. in Educational Administration at Claremont Graduate School in 1987.

Her professional experience includes elementary school teaching, acting principal, school psychologist and associate professor at California State University, Los Angeles and Long Beach. Having mastered Japanese and French at the University of Maryland, Senator Watson taught gifted children in Okinawa and France.

In 1975, Senator Watson was elected to the Board of Education for the Los Angeles Unified School District, the first elected African-American to serve in this capacity. She is often remembered for her dedicated attempt to desegregate the Los Angeles Unified School District.

Senator Watson made history in 1978 when she became the first African-American woman elected to the California State Senate. Her legislative agenda has consistently addressed the health, economic, and legal concerns of women. She is committed to the interests of the disabled and the civil rights of minorities. She has carried pioneering legislation on domestic violence, hate crimes, rape, child-care service, reproductive health, medical ethics and access to health care.

In the Senate, she serves as chairperson of the Health and Human Services Committee. For nine years (1983-1992) she has been elected chairperson of the California Legislative Black Caucus, a group of black elected officials in the Legislature. She founded the National Organization of Black Elected Legislators/Women (NOBEL/Women), a coalition of black women state legislators across the country.

Among her many awards are the 1992 "Legislator of the Year" from the National Organization for Women; the 1982 and 1992 "Senator of the Year" from the California Trial Lawyers and the 1989 "Outstanding Legislator" from the California League of Conservation voters.

Diane E. Watson

California State Senate
28th Senatorial District

Diane E. Watson

["Crack: Crisis in the African American Community," speech given to the Southern Christian Leadership Conference of Greater Los Angeles and University of Southern California School of Medicine, February 1990.]

I must thank you, ladies and gentlemen, for inviting me here tonight. I am so heartened that you are here and that this conference has been called. Tonight, I will not bid you good evening. For it is not. It is, in fact, far too late in the day for us to be talking about what I want, what I feel compelled to talk with you about tonight—crack—and its effect on African-Americans. It is late for us to be talking at all, instead of doing.

Our morning has slipped by. Afternoon, the high tide of the day, is gone. We stand in the deepness of night. Walking into darkness, we peer and stumble, blinking to recover sight as hope and opportunity slip away from us. There is nothing beautiful about this night. I cannot bid you good evening for morning may not come.

It is impossible to exaggerate our plight. Let's get the horrifying figures and statistics out of the way now, quickly, so that we can spend the rest of our time during this conference discussing solutions.

Although African-Americans make up only 12 percent of the nation's population, we are 55 percent of those treated in emergency rooms for cocaine-related illnesses. Black males now comprise more than 50 percent of male drug-related deaths, up from 30 percent in 1984. In 1987, 231 of every 10,000 live births at Harbor-UCLA Medical Center were cocaine-exposed babies. Oakland reported that between 1983 and 1987 there was a fourfold increase in the number of pregnant mothers who admitted to drug-use during pregnancy.

Drugs and crime go hand-in-hand. By now, we must all know that homicide is the leading cause of death among young black men. In predominantly black Washington, D.C., 57 percent of murders were drug-related, up from 17 percent in 1985, and over the same time period, the annual number of homicides rose from 148 to 228. In 1987, 39 percent of youth held in custody were black. In 1986, 54 percent of state prison inmates reported that they were under the influence of drugs, alcohol, or both at the time they committed the offense for which they were doing time. By 1987, when crack was much less readily available than now, 80 percent of all state prisoners, and nearly 83 percent of youth in long-term, state-run juvenile facilities had used illegal drugs. Half of those sentenced for robbery or burglary were daily drug users. The typical prison inmate first used drugs at age fifteen, and became a habitual user of a "major" drug by age 18, but as of 1986, blacks began such usage two years later than white inmates. I would be much surprised if that gap has not been closed since the wide availability of cheap cocaine in the form of crack. In 1987, fully 38 percent of juveniles in state custody began using drugs before age 12, right around the time they entered junior high school. Thirty percent of drug-using inmates will participate in substance abuse programs. When released, two-thirds will eventually be re-incarcerated for drug-related offenses. In L.A. County, most of them will be black.

The numbers change, grow, worsen hourly. The line at the bottom of the ledger reads *zero*. All of our talk, all of our delays, all of our blame-shifting total up to naught. We are deep in the red. And the red is the color of blood. Black blood.

Although few reliable statistics are yet available on crack cocaine, we know its effects. It's a whirlwind ride on a roller coaster with no brakes. Let's imagine, for a moment, how it happens:

"Picture yourself taking your first hit of crack. It feels good—so good that your body cries out for another hit. But every hit is going to cost you...First, your car. Next, your job. Then, your house. Your crack addiction is so powerful that you wind up homeless, on the streets, within six months after your first hit, you have given up everything for a hit of crack—including your family, which has sought shelter from or been consigned to the custody of the state.

"You don't eat or sleep right anymore. You don't go outside anymore because the sunlight hurts. Time no longer means anything. Your chances of contracting AIDS or other intravenous or sexually transmitted diseases are greatly increased because the only people who will hang out with you anymore are those who are strung out like you. The *sole* purpose of your existence is to find some crack and smoke it, and then find some *more* crack and smoke that." Edward Robinson wrote that description of the life of a "crackhead" in the San Francisco Weekly.

What is crack? A little bit of heaven and a whole lot of hell, only assaulting its victims after it has seduced them. Chemically, says the Los Angeles Times, crack is "turbo-charged cocaine in smokable rock form. It jolts the brain with a charge that sends the senses reeling. Users want to jump up and down and run a one-minute mile—but they often just sit there, hearts racing, sometimes so fast that they go into cardiac arrest."

Psychologically, crack is the meltdown of pain. Ecstatic oblivion. When dreaming feels so much better than waking, why not sleep forever? The sense of power experienced through crack is so intense precisely because it is severed from all motivation. Pure undischarged energy. Crack is being able to feel good without having to be good or to do good. It is this sensation of limitless potential set free from any need or desire to act that is irresistible. Understandably so: power never put to the test can never become failure.

Crack is a short-term insurance policy against failure. And a long-term guarantee of failure. Throughout this day, you will be attempting to assess the impact of cocaine on the lives of African-Americans in order to identify feasible solutions. I urge that, in the process, you focus upon the multi-layered, interlinking problems which center on the fear of failure. That fear afflicts those who use drugs and we who, too often, fear to help them.

Fear has Sacramento in its grip. I could rattle off a variety of bills worming their way through legislative committees and programs squirreled away in obscure departments in the state, all set up to make it look as though the Legislature and governor are tackling the problem of substance abuse. But as I have already said, it is far too late in the day for me to lead you on a wild goose chase. I don't mean that there is no hope in Sacramento. Some of us do keep trying to wake up our colleagues on this issue, and while others continue to doze, we try to put through a pilot program desperately needed in South Central Los Angeles or to help an innovative anti-drug community-based organization in Alameda County. I am working on two bills, one of which would facilitate increasing the number of drug treatment centers, both in-patient and out-patient, while the other would establish an academy of home health care workers who could provide substance abuse counseling and treatment.

But for the most part I do not think that our best hope this year lies in the state Capitol. Effective programs cost money. Raising money requires lifting Proposition 13 limits, modifying the Gann limit, and possibly raising taxes. Even if this were not an election year, the governor exercises an override-proof veto which, in his last two years in office, he has shown no hesitance to wield like a meat cleaver. Politicians know that Californians want drug usage, gang violence and crime brought down. But the pollsters keep telling us that they aren't willing to pay for it.

Some of my Republican colleagues have figured out that the best government solution to the problem of crack is the cheapest: containment. So long as the problem has not struck rural California, and is not yet at crisis proportions in the suburbs, they are convinced that no one really minds if the drug traffic wreaks its destruction in the inner cities of Los Angeles, Oakland, San Francisco and San Diego.

Too many Californians have decided that the smart thing to do is not to help solve the problems which afflict our cities, but to protect oneself and one's lifestyle from their impacts.

The process of *cocooning* has begun: people are choosing to wrap themselves and their families up tightly in whatever advantages, resources and privileges they have been able to accumulate. The best schools, the "good" neighborhoods, the high-paying jobs, the least-polluted environments, even the least-congested streets are being perceived as commodities too scarce to be shared, too precious *not* to be hoarded. **NIMBY**, the Not-In-My-Back-Yard syndrome, is the new bunker mentality of urban communities. Instead of joining the white flight to suburbia, many urban Anglos have decided to hermetically seal off their neighborhoods from the city around them in order to protect their quality of life.

While some of my colleagues in Sacramento have seen this trend as the indelible handwriting on the wall, others are rejoicing at it, joining the cheering section. Among these is George Deukmejian. As an advocate of the you-got-yourselves-into-this-mess-so-get-yourselves-out school of rugged individualism, the governor and his allies are determined to ignore the diminished quality of life we all experience when neglect is adopted as a political policy in our urban centers. If he is succeeded by another Republican, who will also be veto-proof, I frankly see little chance of progress in our war on crack.

As crime and violence escalate in association with crack use, I think we must expect more and more demands for a punitive approach to addressing the problem. While this worries me somewhat, I am convinced that the "anti-everything" forces will find that they have painted themselves into a corner, by whipping up the thirst for revenge among our citizenry. More police, more prisons, and longer sentences also cost money, and prisons must be located somewhere. By encouraging their constituents to believe that they can have all the benefits of life in a boom state, with none of the costs, they will discover that they have whetted a public appetite they cannot feed and yet dare not refuse. They have been guilty in their suburban districts of the very thing they accuse Democrats of doing in the inner cities: fostering the notion that individuals and communities are entitled to benefits they won't pay for. Irresponsible themselves, Republican leaders have encouraged irresponsibility among the voters, and when it becomes evident that no one can have their cake and eat it too, they will themselves be eaten by angry **NIMBY**-ites.

Meanwhile, where are we to turn for help against substance abuse? First of all, we must continue to fight: for attention, for resources, for money in Sacramento, in Washington and in City Hall. I pledge to continue to wage that battle on behalf of African-Americans and all Californians. But I also believe that if we look within the black community, we will find options we have not yet considered and answers to questions we have been afraid to ask.

The key lies in understanding the fear of failure I spoke of earlier, and in not deluding ourselves about the nature and depth of the crisis we face.

I am still trying to absorb that statistic, that nearly 40 percent of juvenile offenders began to use drugs before the age of 14. Forget the adult addicts for a moment. What could make a child turn to drugs? What could a girl or boy know about themselves at that age to make such a choice seem realistic?

Environment has much to do with it. Gangs are everywhere, and the pressure they bring to bear on youngsters for conformity is as casual as child's play, as calculated as the cultivation of new customers, and as cold as death by a semi-automatic. The need to be accepted, for safety and for sanity, is strongest when you hover on the verge of adulthood.

Kids at risk may benefit from counseling, diversion, one-on-one intervention, structured programs, or imposition of discipline. But whatever we come up with must be able to provide or compete with what gangs offer in large doses: personal visibility and non-judgmental acceptance from peers.

The reality is that even in the toughest neighborhoods, in the most drug-saturated schools, the majority of black youngsters do not become gang-bangers, do not sell or use drugs (even if they have occasionally experimented with them) and do not become criminals. We need to take a hard-nosed look at what differentiates those who do from those who don't.

Why do some start and others don't? More specifically, why do so many of *our* people choose to join this downward spiral? It may help to ask why most of us don't. For most Americans, life is a range of options which they have reason to believe can, with care and effort, lead to achievement of much of what makes life worth living. It makes sense to map out a life plan and to stick to it, because if pursued, with a minimum of dead-ends and detours, there is a likelihood that the end will be achieved. The prospect of such material rewards as education, career, affluence, prominence, home ownership, travel, etc. are strong incentives to stay on course.

The person who does not feel these incentives and disincentives has little reason to avoid the immediate social acceptance and pleasure of drugs. There may be complete understanding of the dangers of crack, but no sense that if addiction follows experimentation, *real* life opportunities are thereby forfeited. In order not to succumb to fear of failure, there must be grounds for belief in success.

What happens to so many young black people to stifle development of positive self-esteem? Why do so many find it so difficult to reach down inside and locate the wherewithal to resist the temptation to succumb to crack or other drugs, or to gangs, or crime, or violence? The answers are still emerging. But in conclusion I wish to focus on a piece of history I think African-Americans are often prone to forget, and which I urge you to bear in mind as you tackle the connections between crack and fear of failure.

Since the mid-1960s, American blacks have been fighting not a legal war against segregation, nor an insurmountable economic war against discrimination, but a profound psychological war for our own sense of self-worth.

We are fighting to free ourselves of the *psychological bondage* to which Africans were subjected in this country. It is the damage which results when you distort a people's belief in the cause-and-effect principle of the universe. It is the faith in this principle which motivates achievement and enables self-respect. It is the belief that *effort produces results*. It is the notion that I can get what I want if I work hard enough, smart enough, long enough. It is what teaches a human being to believe in productive labor. It is self-discipline.

When racism teaches a man that he must labor, not for self-improvement, but because it is the unique doom of his race, that man will hate labor and loathe his race. When a woman comes to perceive that no matter how hard she works, she can only marginally improve her lot in life, that woman will come to believe that effort is an evil. When children learn that their status in society will always be determined more by the color of their skin than by their achievements, such children will grow up convinced that achievement is futile. When a culture is ingrained with the concept that there is **no cause-and-effect** relationship between **effort and reward**, that culture will fit its people for survival at the lowest, meanest level of existence, and fail to teach the value of self-discipline.

I submit that as you ponder today how we shall win the war against crack, you will be deciding strategy to win what I dare hope is the final battle in the African-American war against racism. Crack is just Jim Crow in a pipe.

Again, I say: it is late in the day. Use well your time!

Delaine Eastin

A native Californian, Delaine Eastin earned a B.A. from the University of California at Davis and an M.A. in Political Science from the University of California at Santa Barbara. She taught political science for seven years and was employed by the Pacific Telesis Group as a corporate planner. She was twice elected to the City Council of Union City.

In November, 1986, Eastin won the Assembly seat for the 20th District which includes the communities of Fremont, Milpitas, Newark, Sunol and portions of San Jose and Pleasanton. As chair of the Assembly Committee on Education, she has sponsored major legislation to reform the K-12 education system and to expedite school facility development. Her prior accomplishments include a $100 million measure for clean-up of toxic landfills, measures designed to expedite completion of highway projects, expansion of markets for recycled paper, glass and metals, and reorganization of state government agencies for increased efficiency. She successfully carried a $1.9 billion school facilities bond measure, the largest in the history of the state. It was passed by the electorate in June, 1992. She has carried bills to expand and improve libraries in every term in which she has served. One was finally signed into law in 1993.

In addition to her legislative responsibilities, she is former president of the board of CEWAER (California Elected Women's Association for Education and Research), serves on the board of the University of California, Santa Barbara's Alumni Association, the Commission on the Status of Women, the California Coalition for Mathematics, the Workforce California Leadership Board, and the National Board for Professional Teaching Standards.

Delaine Eastin is noted for her spirit of bipartisan cooperation, and her devotion to California's public education system. She was named "Cream of the Freshman Crop," *California Journal*, 1987; "Rookie of the Year," *California Journal*, 1988; "Legislator of the Year," California School Boards Association, 1991; "Legislator of the Year," California Council, American Institute of Architects, 1991, and "Legislator Who is Making a Difference," *Governing* magazine, 1992.

Delaine Eastin is running for the nonpartisan statewide office of superintendent of public instruction and has a June, 1994, primary election.

Delaine Eastin

California State Assembly
20th Assembly District

Delaine Eastin

[Speech given at the graduation ceremonies of the College of Letters and Science, University of California, Davis, June 20, 1992.]

*T*hank you for that kind introduction.

It's a great honor to be welcomed home to the school I love.

This is the place my husband and I came the day he returned from Vietnam. To us, this campus recalled freedom—the time and encouragement to read and think and talk—and to dream about how we might help to make the world a better place.

That's what a great many of us had in mind that warm day in June of 1969 when I graduated from Davis.

We didn't like the status quo, and we made no secret of that. We saw our parents going along to get along. Sometimes it seemed to us they had compromised a lot to get ahead and stay ahead. Children of the Great Depression, our parents seemed to be playing it safe to a fault.

We, by contrast, imagined life as bold, passionate strokes. Bobby Kennedy, I think quoting Shaw, had said: "Some see things as they are and ask why. I see things that never were and ask why not?"

Why couldn't the "powers-that-be" grant full membership in the human family to minorities and women? Why couldn't industry respect the planet's life-support systems? Why wasn't war considered a catastrophic failure on the part of all involved? Why not?

Well, nearly a quarter century has passed. Indeed, the world has changed radically, and my generation played a major role.

But the change was not the one we expected. And our role was not the one we envisioned.

For more than a decade after graduation, we witnessed the ills of society stand up with amazing stubbornness to bold, passionate strokes. By the end of the 70s, it looked like a stalemate. Many became disillusioned. Discouraged. Bored. Idealism should be made of sterner stuff.

In any event, the fateful choice came in the early 1980s. We heard the call of a new movement, new leaders. They too saw things that never were, and asked why not.

Riding high among them was a man that Berkeley invited in 1982 to deliver a commencement address. His name was Ivan Boesky.

Unlike this one will be, his speech was quoted around the world.

"Greed is good," Boesky told Berkeley—in just those words.

Don't be ashamed of greed, he said. Be proud of it. The more greed, the more drive. The more drive, the more done. In the end, he said, the greediest among you will dominate the rest. This is natural and therefore good. Go for the jugular and enjoy it. God bless America, etc., etc., etc.

Well, there was obviously a certain tension between that line of reasoning and the ideals my classmates shared back in 1969.

Our words to live by had come from an artist, John Lennon. He said, "All you need is love." For us, that was the glue around a whole constellation of values—community and compassion, free expression and tolerance, nature and art and friendship.

Why did so many people go over to Boesky's value system?

I think because the "greed is good" people were winning.

Isn't that the test? Who wins? In the marketplace. In opinion polls. In elections.

Well, thankfully, winning isn't supposed to be everything in academia. Here, I'm told, people are still expected to ask not who won, but where is truth?

Boesky got a platform in '82 because the "greed is good" people had launched something really big. A few years later it would be called the longest peacetime economic expansion in history.

Business leaders went on television in the mid-80s bragging that their companies were going to do great things in the marketplace because they had become "lean and mean."

That "lean and mean" stuff always puzzled me. I may not be Peter Drucker, but I have a checkbook. I consider myself a discerning customer—and I take my trade to merchants who are fat and jolly.

I find "lean and mean" attitudes disgusting.

Here's the dictionary definition of "mean." Listen: Destitute of moral integrity. Ignoble. Small-minded. Petty. Offensive. Unaccommodating.

This attracts customers? Gimme a break.

No, ladies and gentlemen. The "lean and mean" baloney had nothing to do with serving customers. Something else was going on.

It was called restructuring and it hit the average working family like a freight train.

Restructuring was supposed to make Americans more competitive against foreign producers. But it played out just like that dictionary definition I just read.

During the longest peacetime expansion in history, 12 million people lost their jobs.

Those who survived were not spared. The number of full-time workers compensated with poverty-level wages increased by one-third, or 10 million people—this during the longest peacetime expansion in history.

Statistics like these have consequences. One-third of nursing home employees in urban areas today hold two full-time jobs. Anyone here ever heard about nursing homes making tragic mistakes?

As for the average worker across the whole economy, the longest peacetime expansion in history saw the average annual wage fall 19 percent.

Now...whenever such great progress is achieved, those who are responsible are well-rewarded.

So the share of national income going to the wealthiest 10 percent rose faster than in any period since World War II.

And—onto the scene, for the first time in nearly a century, came top management pay packages fit for royalty.

A few months ago, the chairman of Coca-Cola went public to defend $80 million in compensation for the work he did last year. He said it was a great year for soda pop, and the credit rightfully went to him.

Some CEOs use the so-called Madonna defense. Madonna got a $60 million deal from Time-Warner, so what's the difference?

The difference, I think, should be obvious to a third grader. Madonna is the whole show and the head of Coca-Cola, whatever he claims, is not. The comparison is bogus on the face of it.

The fact of the matter is that the marketplace is good to CEOs because they run it. End of story.

Who are we kidding?

Now, I think it's necessary to point out here that the greatest peacetime expansion in history was also very good to people who run...universities.

It hurts me to say this. I have spent many constructive hours with the president of this institution discussing the needs of the university. I know him to be completely dedicated to the excellence of UC and I respect him deeply.

However, this is not Wall Street.

During the hearings on university compensation, a spokesman for the Regents said, "Look, you want a great university? You have to pay what the marketplace demands."

Oh, do we?

Gordon Sproul. Ernest Lawrence, Clark Kerr. Emil Mrak. And many others whose names I frankly don't know. But I do know this: they built the finest public university in the world, and they did it for civil servant wages.

Plus—I will grant you—a bonus: society recognized them for what they were: the tenders and guardians of human reason—at the end of the day, perhaps the most important role on earth.

Maybe this is what happened. During the greatest peacetime expansion in history, our national culture—our notions of true and lasting value—cheapened alarmingly.

And in the rotting, it seems that society just stopped granting that bonus of honor to its academic leaders. And so the marketplace, with its unerring sense of such things, stepped into compensate—by increasing their base pay.

So where is the truth? On the liberal side, maybe? I'm sorry to say I'm not betting on it.

Let's not forget that many of my contemporaries who became teachers were among those who—with good motives, I'm sure—sought to free children from arbitrary rules—like grammar.

What counted, they said, was the child's expression. Any idea was just fine. And why sweat the small stuff—like spelling and logic?

That approach to teaching is now being challenged.

I count myself among those who seek improvement by freeing education from the bureaucracy that has traditionally run it. Today's reformers are eager to let innovative teachers freely contribute their ideas. Eager to welcome parents into the schools to help their kids grow.

Do I truly believe in parental involvement, people ask me? Let me put it this way: My dream is the day when parental involvement in education will be the public school equivalent of tuition, forgiven only under compelling circumstances.

I say we'll educate your children for free, but not for nothing. There's a big difference.

We have to send the clear message that parents are responsible for raising their children—in the fullest sense of the term.

But to make that happen, we first have to stop pushing parents to the breaking point. Employed Americans today put in a longer work week than anyplace in the world except Japan.

Even the Japanese government now sees that too much work is a problem, and so has established a Department of Leisure to persuade workers to take more time off.

Granted, progress so far has been minimal. But Japanese leaders say they're serious, and they point with pride to the 12-hour days that have become the norm at the Department of Leisure.

As Herb Caen says: Unclear on the concept.

But look at Europe. They're reasonable people. Six weeks vacation is the standard, and these are sound economies.

The point is this: being there for children is a productive and useful way to spend time, and we have to get that.

We also have to start letting go of what's not working in the classroom—even if it poses a risk for an old guard.

I spend much of my time working with leaders of the stakeholder groups that take part in public education.

These people consider themselves open-minded and progressive.

And yet, if I close my eyes and listen to all the reasons why new ideas are dangerous, I think I'm listening to the bosses of General Motors in 1975 on why American consumers will always reject foreign cars.

So where is the truth?

The "greed is good" people tell me I'm wasting my time. They say education could be reformed in no time at all—by just letting it slip smoothly into the current of the marketplace.

Sure, that's an option. But let's not kid ourselves. When we say it's our policy to leave a set of decisions to the marketplace, we're saying that it's our policy to accept whatever happens.

Let me be clear: whatever happens can be a wonderful miracle. I'm a believer. For the quick and efficient delivery of goods to those who are ready to pay, you can't beat the marketplace.

But the nurturing of a child's mind—is this something we really want to leave to "whatever happens"?

The fault line in the endless debate over public goods versus private goods cuts, however raggedly, across the question of who will be included.

Market solutions naturally cluster people by ability to pay. Nordstrom people shop together. K-Mart people shop together. Salvation Army people, and so forth.

Promoters of free market schools don't like that observation. They don't like it one bit. They assure me that there is lots of concern for the poor among the better-off and that voluntary action would create plenty of scholarships to remedy disparities in opportunity.

I don't believe that.

Maybe in some past era, but not now.

You can tell a lot about America's changing readiness to sacrifice for the sake of the future by comparing the quality of rhetoric that moves a nation in different periods.

When I was your age, a pollster could have asked the whole country to cite one line out of all the presidential speeches they had ever heard—the one that moved them the most—and there is no question in my mind that a vast majority would have quoted the same one:

"Ask not what your country can do for you, ask what you can do for your country."

What was the most recent jewel of rhetoric that moved this nation? We all know what it was: "Read my lips. No new taxes."

Some of you, as you prepare to leave this place, may find that tax cutting, and cost cutting, and job cutting have no power to inspire.

If you'd rather build than cut, then I would advise you to select your mentors with care.

Yes, there are notable exceptions, but on the whole, you should probably be skeptical about listening to my generation. We were the biggest, best educated and most fired-up bunch of dreamers in history.

And—at least to this point—a great disappointment.

Instead, you might think about looking up to some people who, indeed, saw things that never were and asked why not.

Your grandparents.

During the greatest peacetime expansion in history, our country's economic infrastructure rotted.

By contrast, your grandparents built and built and built. The Golden Gate Bridge. The San Francisco Bay Bridge—two local examples—and they built them at the bottom of the Great Depression—when nobody had any money at all.

How? Vision. And heart. And guts.

You want to know what it's like to see things that never were and ask why not? Go seek out one who changed my life—by giving me the chance to attend this university. He is today an old man. His name is Pat Brown. I have seen him recently and I know he would be delighted to talk with you.

Pat Brown was governor of this state when I was a little girl. He envisioned a great state university, vastly expanded to serve a growing state. During his eight years as governor he built one-third of all UC campuses.

His four successors over nearly 30 years have added not one. And during that time the state has doubled in population.

What ever happened to vision like Pat Brown's?

Maybe it's here, among you, waiting to come back into the world. Your country needs it, as never before.

Build commitment to the long-term health of this republic. Build it among yourselves.

And, as for my own generation, let me take the liberty of at least expressing a hope--that if you build it, we will come. Come home to our senses. Come home to a decent and caring future. Come home to America.

God bless you all.

Sunne Wright McPeak

$\mathcal{S}$unne Wright McPeak was first elected to the Board of Supervisors of Contra Costa County in 1978. She was re-elected in 1982, 1986 and 1990. She has served on the board's committees on internal operations, budget, water, medical services, plastics recycling, energy, and the Partnership for a Drug-Free Contra Costa. She has earned a statewide reputation for her expertise on water management.

She has been co-chair of the State Water Conservation Coalition, chair of the Committee for Water Policy Consensus, representing leadership in 12 Bay Area and Delta counties, and is a frequent speaker on water problems and solutions.

She has served as president of the County Supervisors Association of California, as director of the Bay Area Economic Forum and as a member of the State Legislative Council on Nutrition Labeling. Her public work in many areas has been honored by diverse groups: United Way, Soroptimist International, Jaycees, American Society for Public Administration, Rotary International. She was named Honorary Mexican-American of the Year, 1981 by the United Council of Spanish-Speaking Organizations and was given the Silver Spoon Award, 1990, by the Diablo Valley Dietetic Association.

McPeak came to public life with a business and health services background. Raised on a dairy farm in Livingston, California, she has a B.A. degree from the University of California, Santa Barbara and a master's degree in public health from the University of California, Berkeley. Prior to her election as supervisor, she was owner of McPeak Associates, a management consulting firm in human services and on the Board of Directors of the First Nationwide Bank.

In October, 1993, McPeak resigned effective March 31, 1994, from the Contra Costa Board of Supervisors. She is currently the executive director of the Bay Area Economic Forum, a public/private partnership to stimulate the San Francisco Bay Area economy.

Sunne Wright McPeak

Board of Supervisors
Contra Costa County
District 4
(1978-March 1994)

$\mathcal{S}$unne $\mathcal{W}$right $\mathcal{M}$c$\mathcal{P}$eak

["Achieving Consensus on Water Policy," speech given November, 1991.]

$\mathcal{I}$t is not only possible, but it is also essential, that we achieve consensus on water policy in California. The state's economic vitality and environmental quality are at risk.

Fortunately, the ability to achieve consensus is definitely within the grasp of state leaders if they are sincere about addressing the key issues and if they utilize a consensus process to reach agreement. In fact, meeting the state's future water needs for at least the next 20 years is a relatively simple problem technically to solve in comparison to all the other hurdles facing California. What is needed to make this happen is leadership from all sectors of the state that is dedicated to a "New Water Ethic" with a clear vision of the opportunities for consensus. Therein lies the challenge.

Since the defeat of two statewide water measures by the voters in 1982—the Peripheral Canal referendum (Proposition 9) in June and a water management initiative (Proposition 13) in November—it has been evident that the only way to achieve progress on water issues is by building broad-based consensus instead of forcing legislation through a political process. Those elections reflected a new reality in water politics, whereby it is possible for any one region of the state or coalition of interest groups to block all the rest. We can literally checkmate each other on the water chessboard. The result is political gridlock and policy stalemate. However, every time a sincere effort has been made by key parties to reach consensus, progress has been made.

A consensus approach has produced significant accomplishments in water policy during the last decade. Those achievements include: (1) authorization of Los Banos Grandes Reservoir for additional water storage; (2) approval of the Coordinate Operation Agreement (COA) and enactment of HR 3113 to coordinate operations of the State Water Project (SWP) and the federal Central Valley Project (CVP); (3) completion of the "two-agency fish agreement" between the Department of Water Resources and the Department of Fish and Game to mitigate fish losses at the export pumps; (4) agreement for exchange of water between the Metropolitan Water District of Southern California and the Imperial Irrigation District; (5) passage of legislation to reconstruct and maintain Sacramento-San Joaquin Delta levees; (6) agreement for protection of the managed portion of Suisun Marsh; (7) development of a conservation agreement among urban water districts, environmental groups, and other public-interest organizations to implement "best management practices" that will generate approximately one million acre feet annually of additional water supply by the end of the decade; (8) agreement regarding identification of the potential for [generating] 244,000 acre-feet additional fresh water displaced by the year 2000 through water recycling, reuse and reclamation; (9) completion of a citizens' advisory committee report and recommendations on San Joaquin Valley drainage; and (10) passage of the Water Conservation in Landscaping Act and agreement on a model water-efficient landscape ordinance for all cities and counties in California.

Some of the toughest policy questions remain: environmental protections for the San Francisco Bay-Delta Estuary; improved delta transfer facilities; and providing an adequate, reliable, quality water supply for future demands. The next phase of statewide consensus negotiations must deal with all these issues in order to avoid a shortfall in California's water supply by the year 2000.

Agreement will be achieved on meeting California's future water needs only when state leaders understand that the key to consensus is a policy package with a minimum of the following three components: (1) adequate environmental protections for the Bay-Delta Estuary; (2) conservation and efficient use of the existing supply; and (3) construction of water banking facilities to improve delta transfer of exports and to reduce environmental damage. There are several specific elements and implementation steps related to each of these components that must be spelled out and negotiated. However, the opportunity for consensus exists when all three components are addressed concurrently.

This approach will not only resolve the most immediate, difficult issues but it will also produce benefits for all regions of the state. It is important to note that the consensus package does not include consideration of a Peripheral Canal or any other isolated delta transfer facility at this time. Resurrection of the Peripheral Canal concept at this point in negotiations will result in confrontation and will delay consensus. The non-isolated water banking proposal is a superior policy and engineering approach for achieving consensus in this decade.

Finally, it must be underscored that statewide consensus will be achieved sooner with strong leadership from the governor, his administration, and the Legislature. They are wise to encourage and support the current consensus efforts that have been initiated outside of the formal state government structure. It is essential that the key interest groups and stakeholders come to agreement among themselves before state policy can be successfully adopted and implemented. But strong, aggressive leadership from the governor in partnership with the Legislature to facilitate the consensus process would produce significant water policy agreement in the immediate future. And that would be a great benefit to California's economy and environment.

The context for consensus is created by the adoption of a "New Water Ethic" which establishes a dramatic departure from previous water practices and past water politics. Put simply, a New Water Ethic realizes that water is a limited natural resource that cannot be wasted and recognizes the need to preserve and to protect the environment for future generations. A New Water Ethic reflects a fundamental shift in thinking which rejects huge water development projects as the only way to meet future water needs, and which advocates maximizing the efficient use of the current supply as an essential part of the equation. It sets forth the prerequisite that environmental safeguards be enacted before more water is diverted or developed for consumptive uses; and it delineates the principle that new water development projects be approved only if they are environmentally safe and economically sound.

Historically, controversies have erupted over water when it was perceived that one region would benefit at the expense of another, or when the environment was being sacrificed for the profit of the economy. A New Water Ethic defines the "common ground" upon which negotiations can take place to reach consensus about meeting future water needs. It brings together all the stakeholders and interested parties in a new relationship built upon a different premise that avoids the basic conflicts of the past.

Embracing a New Water Ethic (or its policy equivalent) is an essential first step towards consensus. Achieving consensus, however, depends also on the ability of state leaders to accurately identify the opportunities for agreement and the appropriate sequence for seizing them. An opportunity for consensus exists when stakeholders are willing to concede something desired by others in order to gain more in return than is assured by the status quo. An opportunity will become a reality only if all stakeholders win. Further, the sequence in which issues are addressed can often be very critical. It is usually wise to tackle the relatively easier or less controversial issues first in order to build trust and a track record of success.

Over the last decade the successful consensus efforts have worked through a series of important issues, demonstrating that agreement on water policy is possible with the right approach. Generally, those efforts have addressed how to make the current water system work more efficiently. The issues yet to be resolved are the toughest because they are either the most difficult technically (involving supply reallocations or new construction) or the most controversial (dealing with the delta transfer facilities). However, we can no longer avoid coming to terms with these issues. Failure to do so will result in continuing degradation of the Bay-Delta Estuary and the prospect of shortfalls in water supply by the end of the decade. Therefore, the next round of statewide consensus negotiations must address a certain set of remaining issues, including: ecological deterioration of the Bay-Delta Estuary, improved delta transfer facilities to mitigate impacts of the current export system, and reliability of an adequate, quality water supply to meet future demands. Only when all of these problems are addressed simultaneously is there a potential for trade-offs in negotiations such that all parties can have a "win" and gain more than they have by doing nothing.

The framework for reaching consensus on water policy to resolve the above problems must contain at least the following three components: (1) adequate environmental protections for the Bay-Delta Estuary; (2) conservation and efficient use of the existing supply; and (3) construction of water banking facilities to improve delta transfer of exports and to reduce environmental damage. Each of these three components encompass several elements and implementation steps, but it is the combination of these three components that creates the opportunity for consensus and the possibility that all parties win.

Why is the combination of the above three components in a policy package key to achieving consensus? The most important "bottom line" issue for the bay-delta region is protection of the Bay-Delta Estuary, the foundation of the area's ecology and economy. The most pressing concern for Southern California is meeting future water demands with a reliable water supply of acceptable quality. In the past, the struggle resulting from each region independently pursuing these two goals has been perceived as a "sum zero game." It was thought that if Southern California expanded their water supply, it meant more exports out of the delta and less water for the environment. Likewise, it was assumed that increased environmental protections for the Bay-Delta Estuary meant a reduced water supply for Southern California and the San Joaquin Valley. But this is not necessarily the case. If additional water can be generated from conservation and more efficient use of the existing supply, then some future demand can be met without increased delta exports. Also, water banking holds the prospect of actually expanding the "water pie" in the delta so that both environmental protections can be enhanced and the water supply increased. However, new facilities must be constructed in order to implement water banking. But there will never be consensus on any new delta facilities until adequate bay-delta environmental protections are guaranteed and unless the efficient use of the current developed water supply is assured. Hence, all three components (bay-delta protections, conservation and efficient use, and water banking) must be addressed simultaneously and combined in a policy package in order to achieve consensus.

Note that this approach also avoids the tired debated of "conservation versus construction." The reality is we need to do both. We must implement all feasible conservation measures not only to fulfill the spirit of a New Water Ethic but also to enable us to meet future demands until new construction projects are completed. And we need new construction not only to meet additional future demands but also to mitigate the negative impacts of the current delta export system.

The following describes in more detail the specific elements and implementation steps of the three components.

There is no state law that pertains directly to environmental protection for the Bay-Delta estuary. The Delta Protection Act addresses only the delta. It is time that state law acknowledges the reality of nature, namely that the San Francisco Bay/Sacramento-San Joaquin Delta Estuary is a dynamic ecosystem that must be protected as a whole. Therefore, it is critical that the cornerstone of sufficient and complete environmental protections for the estuary be the enactment of a law (or provision in a policy package) that establishes "it is the policy of the state and all of its officers to protect and preserve all reasonable and beneficial uses of the Bay-Delta Estuary." The law should further require that the Department of Water Resources (DWR) manage the State Water Project in a manner that mitigates the negative impacts of its operation. Although the exact wording of a bay-delta protection act is open for discussion, the essence of this concept must be embedded in state law. While scientific data over time may alter the specific standards or regulations imposed to comply with the law, this approach is critical because it establishes as a matter of law that the Bay-Delta Estuary shall not be destroyed and conveys the notion that there is a point beyond which delta exports cannot be increased, regardless of other competing interests.

A Bay-Delta Estuary protection act must be enacted at least in statute. Advocates for the bay-delta region would also prefer to include this kind of environmental protection in the state constitution along with the area-of-origin and county-of-origin laws.

Further, in order to reach consensus on construction of facilities that would have the potential of exporting more water out of the delta, it is essential that the State Water Resources Control Board (SWRCB) be required to set adequate and complete water quality standards for the delta and bay before the export levels are actually increased. The new standard must provide for increased spring flows, reduced pumping in critical months, appropriate temperature controls, and improved salinity objectives. It is important to note that consensus on facilities does not depend on first setting the new standards but rather on requiring that new facilities cannot be operated for the purposes of increasing export levels until the new standards have been set by the SWRCB and are in force. Articulating this kind of "sequencing" for elements of a policy package helps facilitate consensus.

The biggest fear related to any new delta facilities, isolated or non-isolated, is the prospect of taking more water out of the system at the wrong times. So it is essential that key environmental safeguards be adopted to guarantee that any facility will be operated properly.

There are several important elements in this component of a policy package. They include: (a) implementation of urban conservation programs as encompassed in the "Best Management Practices" (BMP) agreement; (b) construction of water recycling and reuse projects to generate at least 244,000 acre-feet additional fresh water displaced by the year 2000; (c) enactment of water marketing to encourage and facilitate voluntary transfers; (d) implementation of efficient agricultural irrigation practices, including the establishment of goals or targets for system-wide conservation or efficiency; (e) adoption of water pricing reforms to reduce huge subsidies, particularly with water; and (f) retirement of agricultural lands with a severe drainage and toxic contamination problem.

It is estimated that these conservation and water efficiency measures could generate between 1.5 million and 2 million acre-feet annually by the end of the decade. Not only would that provide significant additional supply, but agreement on these conservation measures sets the stage for reaching consensus on delta facilities.

Another opportunity to potentially free up considerable amounts of water for urban uses is renegotiation of the now-expiring 40-year federal water contracts. Shortening the term of the contract and revising the price to more accurately reflect costs will encourage farmers to make different choices about the most economical use of water. Farmers will make economically based decisions resulting in either increased conservation or voluntary transfers.

No discussion of the efficient use of water involving agricultural conservation would be complete without addressing the issue of groundwater management. The current groundwater overdrafting in many farming areas cannot be allowed to continue in the long-term. Therefore, there must be true, overall agricultural water conservation. It will not be acceptable to decrease use of surface supplies only to trigger increased groundwater pumping, causing a greater overdraft. A program must be adopted to reduce the average annual groundwater overdraft over the next 20 years. Innovative conjunctive use programs coupled with groundwater aquifer recharging can be used to address this problem.

Further, although water marketing and voluntary transfers from agriculture to urban uses are viable elements of the efficient use component, caution must be exercised not to inadvertently fallow the most productive agricultural soils in California on a permanent basis. In particular, Class I and II soils (and other significant lands) should be regarded as valuable natural resources and should be protected from urbanization for at least the next two decades. If this position is adopted as policy for the state, then a sufficient amount of water must be retained for agricultural use to assure that the best soils can be successfully cultivated.

Water banking involves building surface and underground storage facilities south of the delta to capture water during periods of high rainfall and huge runoffs when it is truly surplus to the needs of the bay-delta estuarine system. After adequate bay-delta protections and standards are enacted, this would be excess to the ecological requirements of the estuary. Today there is not the capability of "banking" or capturing these surplus waters at peak runoff periods because adequate transfer and storage facilities simply do not exist. Now, pumping occurs on a more constant, year-round basis most years without the flexibility of regulating the pumping to the wetness of the year. With water banking, the pumps could be turned off during crucial months to increase spring outflows and to eliminate reverse flows when fish are spawning. This could be done without decreasing annual exports because the physical facilities would be able to capture the surplus water at other times during the year. The surplus water captured during wet months would also be higher quality, low in chlorides and virtually free of bromides. Further, there is a great likelihood that water banking will produce a new increment of water on the order of 250,000 to 500,000 acre-feet in normal to wet years. This can be done at the same time that environmental protections are strengthened. In this regard, water banking is the linchpin of consensus for both policy and plumbing.

Water banking is a non-isolated facilities proposal for improving delta transfers by widening south delta channels, strengthening levees, installing additional pumps, and constructing Los Banos Grandes Reservoir and Kern Water Bank. Water banking is a superior alternative to the isolated transfer approach of a Peripheral Canal because it accomplishes the same objective without separating the incentives for Southern California to protect the estuary from those of the bay-delta region. Unlike a Peripheral Canal or other isolated transfer facility, water banking maintains a non-isolated "common pool" of water in the delta such that Southern California and San Joaquin exporters have an interest in protecting the Bay-Delta Estuary in order to preserve the quality of water exported.

Proponents of the Peripheral Canal argue for an isolated transfer facility citing allegedly greater concerns about trihalomethanes (THMs) and earthquakes associated with a non-isolated through-delta system. But close analysis of these issues neutralizes the argument for a Peripheral Canal as a preferred engineering solution.

Trihalomethanes are formed when chlorine used in the treatment process combines with organic material in the water. Peripheral Canal promoters emphasize the organics in the delta and gloss over the fact that the Peripheral Canal would be an unlined 43-mile channel, leaving water to pick up organics as it goes through the canal and is stored in earthen terminal reservoirs prior to treatment. Thus, THMs are not eliminated with a Peripheral Canal. Therefore, treatment processes must be installed that will remove THMs and meet anticipated stricter water quality standards, regardless of the kind of delta transfer facility used.

Supporters of the Peripheral Canal also predict that some day an earthquake will destroy the delta channel network creating an inland saltwater sea. They concede that such an earthquake would also damage a Peripheral Canal, but they contend that an isolated channel could be rebuilt more easily than the delta levee system. The problem with this argument is that it is based on the notion that we should abandon the delta island levee system as we know it today and accept the eventual destruction of the bay-delta estuarine ecology. That is not a rational premise upon which to promulgate water policy. It also ignores the function of the existing island levee system in maintaining an estuarine environment. The delta islands and their levees are essentially "place holders" in the estuary, taking up space that otherwise would have to be occupied by fresh water in order to maintain an estuarine system. Thus, the delta levee system has an important function in conserving fresh water. So, even with a non-isolated transfer facility scheme, the levees would have to be maintained unless it is the policy of the state to let the delta estuary become a saltwater environment in the event of an earthquake. It is prudent ecological policy to reconstruct and maintain a strong levee system capable of withstanding severe seismic activity, regardless of whether an isolated or non-isolated transfer facility is advocated.

Faced with the persistent resistance to a Peripheral Canal, some leaders have suggested a "mini-Peripheral Canal" or small drinking water pipeline around the delta. While this is less threatening than a full-blown Peripheral Canal as approved by the Legislature in 1980, this approach ignores the fact that the current export system is destroying the delta and the status quo is not acceptable. So even if a mini-Peripheral Canal or pipeline were built, other facilities (such as water banking) would also have to be constructed to mitigate the negative impacts of the existing export system. The question then arises: Why not implement the non-isolated water banking approach and evaluate its operation before resurrecting the Peripheral Canal controversy again?

Water banking has the ability to enhance environmental protections, protect the fisheries with increased spring outflows and reduced reverse flows, improve water quality and increase the amount of water available for export in normal to wet years. It also has the distinct political advantage of providing a way to improve delta transfer facilities with the least amount of opposition.

When consensus is reached among statewide leaders and organizations, the agreements should be implemented and ratified through a variety of mechanisms. Appropriate vehicles for institutionalizing the consensus agreements include: enactment of legislation (sponsored by the governor and authored by a bipartisan cross-section of the Legislature); ratification of the legislation and approval of any required financing by the voters in a ballot measure; incorporation of the plan by the SWRCB in the bay-delta decision; voluntary agreements (such as the urban conservation BMP agreement); and amendments to the SWP and CVP contracts.

There are real opportunities for water policy consensus in the immediate future as outlined above. However, it should be underscored that California also needs a comprehensive, statewide growth management program that requires (among other things) sufficient water supply be available before new growth is approved. It is in this context that the greatest consensus on water policy can be achieved.

California must have a reliable water supply to support its economic viability. And there must be aggressive protection of the environment to assure the Golden State's quality of life. These two goals cannot be met unless there is progress on meeting the state's future water needs. However, there will be no progress until statewide consensus is achieved on water policy.

In concept, the path to consensus for California water policy is relatively simple and straightforward. However, a simple concept should not be confused with an easy process. Stakeholders must be prepared to give up a little to gain a lot; they must negotiate in sincerity to assure a "win" for all sectors and regions of the state. The framework for water policy consensus involves three essential components: (1) environmental protections for the Bay-Delta Estuary; (2) conservation and efficient use of the existing supply; and (3) water banking facilities. The vital catalyst to achieving consensus is courageous and skillful leadership. If ever there was an issue in need of leadership, it is this. If ever there was a time, it is now.

Sandra Smoley

Sandra R. Smoley was appointed as secretary of the Health and Welfare Agency by Governor Pete Wilson in October of 1993. Smoley is a member of the governor's Cabinet and serves as his chief advisor on health and social service policy. The agency employs more than 42,000 employees and has a budget of $36 billion.

Previously, Smoley served as secretary of the State and Consumer Services Agency where she managed an agency of 15,000 employees and a budget of almost $700 million. Smoley came to the state with extensive experience in local government.

She was the first woman elected to the Board of Supervisors of Sacramento County in 1972; she was re-elected four times; she was chair of the Board of Supervisors for most of those years. She has been president of the County Supervisors' Association of California and president of the National Association of Counties. President Ronald Reagan appointed her to the Advisory Commission on Federalism, his Task Force on Food Assistance and the Advisory Commission on Intergovernmental Relations.

She has served on many regional and local advisory boards: California State University at Sacramento; University of Southern California; the School of Nursing of CSUS; the Robert A. Taft Institute of Government; Sacramento Area Special Olympics. She has been the campaign chair and president of the Board of Directors of the United Way of Greater Sacramento.

Many honors and awards have been given to her: County Taxpayer's League "Elected Official of the Year;" Building Industry Association "Friend of Housing Award, 1990;" the Foster Grandparent Association Award, Sacramento County Black Employees Award, and the American Cancer Society's Personal Courage Award.

Born in Spirit Lake, Iowa, Smoley came to California in 1961 after taking a Bachelor of Science degree in Nursing from the University of Iowa; she did post-graduate studies in economics and management at CSUS and participated in the Harvard Program for Senior Executives in State and Local Government in the John F. Kennedy School of Government.

Sandra Smoley

Board of Supervisors
Sacramento County
(1972-1992)

Sandra Smoley

[Breast cancer speech given May 10, 1992.]

*I*t's a pleasure to be with all of you today. When I was invited to be your guest speaker, I was told I would be with a group where the majority of women have had breast surgery. If this is the case, then we all have a lot in common.

It has been seven years, almost to the day, since I was told I had cancer in both breasts. I felt the shock that anyone would feel when told of the quiet, unfelt invader in my body.

No woman will ever forget where she was when it was confirmed that she had breast cancer. I was in the conference room next to my office with a group of residents who were irate over the installation of a stop sign in their neighborhood. My secretary pulled me out of the meeting to take a call from my doctor. I got the confirmation from him and had to go back in the meeting—somehow the issue of a stop sign seemed so insignificant when compared to a real health problem. That's how you learn not to sweat the small stuff.

Because of my position as an elected official in Sacramento County, I knew that my operation would not be a quiet event shared only with family and close friends. My family, my office staff, and I, accepted the fact that the cancer was there even before we received the official confirmation. We knew my schedule would obviously require revision, and indeed, it did.

We worked harder and longer than ever, realizing that once I did go public with the issue, we would hear from friends and constituents. We were prepared when the news broke—but none of us realized the magnitude of friendship and support that would be coming in. It was overwhelming!

I received approximately 2,500 cards, letters, or calls with beautiful words of encouragement from people of all ages who took time to write or call. I also received 250 beautiful floral arrangements. It was an overwhelming experience for me personally and for my family members and staff. We were suddenly included in that wide group of people who had dealt with the disease—and the thoughtful expressions of kindness from the community will be remembered by all of us forever.

Some other support came from groups such as the American Cancer Society, the volunteers of Encore, and Reach for Recovery. I now serve on the Sharing Place Board, a lovely environment at Sutter Hospital, built for youngsters undergoing cancer treatment at the hospital. Reach for Recovery is an excellent program where a breast cancer person visits patients. And I am on the Board of Directors of the American Cancer Society.

I have been interviewed on radio and television talk shows and in newspaper and magazine feature stories. I have tried to address as many women and their families as possible concerning the issue of breast cancer.

Isn't it wonderful that we now talk about breast cancer out in the open and it is no longer an embarrassment to people?

Since my surgery, I have also had the opportunity to counsel other women I work with on a daily basis who are diagnosed as having breast cancer. I have counseled women I know well and women I met only because they called and asked for support during this emotional and critical time in their lives.

I think an important issue that needs to be addressed is the time frame for healing. My recovery was quick; however, every woman is going to react in her own individual manner when told she has cancer. No woman should ever be criticized because she either recovered too quickly or did not improve quickly enough.

I have been blessed with a supportive husband and my children are grown. If I were not married, or if I had the awesome responsibility of raising youngsters alone, my situation would obviously have been different. Each woman must make her own decisions regarding a mastectomy. I trust other women enough to give them the opportunity to react in the way best for them with no judgment on my part at all. No woman's recovery time should ever be held up to compare to mine—nor mine to hers.

My parents taught me a feeling of self-worth and confidence from my earliest childhood days. My mother's motto is, "Don't stew until you have something to stew about."

Their nurturing and love throughout my life gave me courage to face the unknown head on, and this attitude was a tremendous benefit to me when I was told about the possibility of cancer.

Some of the women in this room have undergone surgery as I did or may be facing it in the future. Please don't burden them with time frames for healing; offer the same encouragement and support I was offered by so many fine people.

As I reflect over the past year, I am aware of the obvious and subtle changes in my life. The obvious are shared by other mastectomy patients—some involve changes in clothes styles, undergarment fittings, and learning to adjust to changes in the contours of our bodies.

Subtle changes involve personal reactions to events and decisions we face every day. I am not the type of person who sweats the small stuff anyway, but after the cancer ordeal, I really put things in their proper perspective. Cancer concerns me and it concerns you.

As a team, we can offer emotional and financial support and encouragement to cancer patients. We can address the issue of cancer and know that our knowledge and support will not only help us but will help those family members or friends who become afflicted. We can look with pride to the inroads made in cancer research and we can look to the future with hope—for the day will come when a cure is found.

The real crusaders for early detection of breast cancer and cures will be those women who have experienced the disease.

Where do you go from here? I can sum it up in two words: get involved.

Get women elected to office.

Get involved with groups such as the American Cancer Society and the Reach for Recovery Program. Through Reach for Recovery, I learned small but very significant points that were not covered during medical consultations. Facts such as: don't carry a purse on my shoulder and where to have blood taken.

If you or any woman you know is still under the notion that breasts on a woman are important to her femininity—forget that misconception.

It's sad to note that there is still a segment of our society that is breast-oriented. I can't tell you the number of people who have asked my husband if my surgery has affected our relationship. My husband and I both feel that having breasts isn't the most important thing in life—the most important thing in life is your good health and how you feel about yourself.

I have elected not to have reconstructive surgery and that suits my husband just fine. However, some men are not that understanding and many women have shared with me their confusion and deep hurt over a man leaving them because their breasts were removed. It's pathetic but true.

Women have to be careful not to let this type of thinking contaminate their own good feelings about themselves and they can't afford to give a flicker of thought to avoiding self-examinations and mammograms because of what they fear might be found. I have always had a positive mental attitude and I'm firmly convinced that our thoughts affect our body's good health.

The American Cancer Society has excellent brochures that are free for the asking that cover what foods may help you reduce your cancer risk—more fresh vegetables, fresh fruits, more fiber, less fat, less salt-cured and smoked foods and more variety in your diet is important.

Become an expert on breast cancer. Encourage your family members, neighbors and friends to increase their awareness of breast cancer and how its early detection can make it possible to cure 97 percent of detected cases; 97 percent is an impressive and positive figure!

I've made it, and you can too—and it's our duty to raise the consciousness level of everyone we know, so others can make it in the future.

Thank you.

Susan Golding

Susan Golding received her B.A. in government and international relations from Carleton College, and an M.A. in romance philology from Columbia University, where she did graduate studies in the School of International Affairs. She taught as a Ph.D. fellow at Emory University and studied at the Sorbonne, Paris. She was associate editor of the Journal of International Affairs, Columbia University, and an instructor at Emory University as well as at San Diego City College and San Diego Miramar College.

She began public service with an appointment to the City Council of San Diego in January, 1981, and was re-elected by a 68 percent city-wide majority later that year. Governor George Deukmejian appointed her the deputy secretary of the Business, Transportation and Housing Agency for the state of California, (March, 1983, to January, 1984). In 1984, she was elected to the San Diego County Board of Supervisors; was re-elected in 1988 and became chair of the board in 1989. She became mayor of San Diego in 1992.

She has worked on civic projects in the fields of ecology, education, government planning and finance, health, transportation, clean water and water reclamation, among others.

She serves on the Republican State Central Committee of the California Republican Party, is a member of the Republican Eagles, Charter 100, served on Governor-Elect Wilson's Transition Advisory Council, and was co-chair of the Committee for the Presidency, George Bush Media Fund, California.

She has received numerous awards and honors, including "1992 Woman of the Year" from the United States-Mexico Foundation; "Supervisor of the Year, 1991" from the San Diego Vietnam Veterans; the Peggy Howell Champion Award from the Friends of County Animal Shelters, 1991, and the Alice Paul Award from the National Women's Political Caucus, 1987.

Susan Golding

Mayor, City of San Diego

Susan Golding

[Speech given at the opening of her campaign headquarters,
San Diego, California, September 12, 1992]

Thank you all for being here. This is an important occasion for me, because it symbolizes my commitment to being mayor for *all* San Diegans.

There are reporters here today, and they need to know how you feel. So speak up and tell me...

— Does City Hall care about your problems?

— Are you getting a fair break when you need financing to buy or improve your homes and businesses?

— Is City Hall taking care of crime in your neighborhoods?

Well, let me tell you something today. *I* care.

I received a phone call from a student at a local adult high school recently. She said she was being racially harassed, and she said no one at the school would help her.

Now, county supervisors aren't in charge of schools, and neither is the mayor. But there *is* a thing called *moral persuasion*.

I contacted the Board of Education and expressed my concerns. The student called back a few days later to tell me that school officials had suddenly started paying attention to her problem.

To me, that's what being mayor is all about.

This community faces a number of problems. But I think they're all related, in one way or another, to the issue of economic development.

Today, I want to announce an inner-city "Marshall Plan" to help you and your neighbors rebuild and revitalize the southern half of this city.

School drop-outs, youth crime, and drugs are problems throughout the city, but they are particularly acute in this community.

With youth unemployment running at nearly 50 percent, the prospects for a young person finishing high school are extremely dim.

We have to build an economy in this community that provides job training and employment opportunities that offer an alternative to gangs and drugs.

Government alone can't accomplish that. As Mayor, I want to help *you and your neighbors* rebuild this community.

I want to work with the school district and private businesses to create high-quality job training centers using empty school facilities. And I want to enlist skilled workers from throughout the city to participate as teachers and pass on their skills to young people who will need those skills to compete for good, high-paying jobs.

I'm going to give the Economic Development Corporation clear marching orders: Attracting new businesses south of I-8 must become their No. 1 priority. And that means more than just paying lip-service!

Access to financing is the first problem any business faces. But there is not a single locally owned bank in this community—no institution committed to making funds available to local businesses.

As a result, much of the money you deposit in the bank is used to finance businesses *outside* your community.

Just one example: There are 160 churches in this community. Together, they collect and deposit between $2 and $3 million in donations every weekend. *All* of that money is deposited in banks headquartered outside this community. *All* of that money could be going to a bank committed to making loans in this community.

I have a proposal: as mayor, I'm going to tell the commercial banks which do business with city government, "If you want to keep doing business with us, I want you to get together and help fund a community development bank for the southern part of our city."

Using federal matching funds, we will create a huge new source of financing for businesses in this community.

Then, combined with appropriate use of enterprise zones and streamlined city permit processing, we will create a climate where business will prosper.

I want a young high school student in this community to be able to look around his or her neighborhood and say, "Wow, look at how well those merchants are doing. I want to start my own business here some day!"

Our neighborhoods are also in need of revitalization. Absentee ownership and limited financing are leading to deteriorated housing.

I have proposed the creation of a "Renaissance Zone" using California Housing Finance Authority funds and city Housing Trust Fund money.

First-time home buyers would receive no-down-payment loans to purchase and rehabilitate deteriorated housing units.

Home ownership is the secret to giving people a stake in the economic and social future of their community. I want to create a whole new generation of home owners in San Diego.

The programs I'm describing—an inner-city "Marshall Plan" and a neighborhood "Renaissance Zone"—use city government as a catalyst. But they rely on you and your neighbors as the engines of change.

That's the kind of city government I want to create in San Diego.

—   De-centralized, with power shifted from City Hall to the neighborhoods.

—   Entrepreneurial, with government as the spark, but with the energy and ideas of the people as the fuel.

Finally, I want to talk to you today about the need to bring people together.

My opponent in this campaign would not be good for our city,

—   Not because many of his theories are harebrained—although many are, and

—   Not because his initiatives would double unemployment and reduce business growth—although experts have estimated they would.

My opponent would be bad for our city because he sees government as a struggle between opposing interests.

He sees it as a war between north and south. He sees it as a war of rich versus poor. He sees it as a war between labor unions and businesses. He sees it as a war between one ethnic group and another.

Now, so far he's been pretty slick in selling that philosophy to voters.

He makes one set of promises to one group and then he goes and makes another set of promises to another group, and most people don't realize he's playing their interests off against somebody else's. Today he's pro-business, tomorrow he's pro-labor. Today he's a rad-talking surfer from the coast and tomorrow he's a jive-talking brother from the streets.

But most of you know that promises like that come home to roost. And when you start treating people in one community like they're in conflict with people in another, eventually you produce real social and political conflict.

Here in San Diego, we don't need academic theories about conflicting interests. We don't need politicians who attempt to manipulate one group against another for personal gain.

What we need is greater respect and concern for our neighbors.

What we need is a sense that *no one* in our city can be *truly* successful until *everyone* in our city has a chance to succeed.

Thank you.

Anne Rudin

Anne Rudin first won election in 1971 to the Sacramento City Council where she served three terms. She was elected mayor in 1983, re-elected in 1987, and did not seek re-election in 1992. Throughout her public service career, she worked to preserve Sacramento's neighborhoods, its architectural and cultural heritage and its quality of life. She serves on the board of directors of the Crocker Art Museum and has supported the arts and cultural activities in their many forms.

As a member of the board of the Sacramento Area Commerce and Trade Organization, she worked to strengthen and diversify Sacramento's economic base and was responsible for creating the city's Office of Economic Development and a minority/women-owned business procurement program. Through her Small Business Roundtable she kept in touch with the needs of the business community.

A longtime civil rights and human rights advocate, Mayor Rudin introduced anti-discrimination ordinances and programs to assist the homeless. She gave special attention to community issues such as drugs, AIDS and child care by forming coalitions of concerned citizens working with public officials to assess the needs and propose courses of action.

She was the first Sacramento mayor to view her city in a global perspective. Under her leadership, international trade, peace and international understanding became municipal concerns. She served on the executive committees of two international conferences of mayors and has been recognized for her efforts to promote peace, nuclear disarmament and a more rational balance between military and human services expenditures.

She has a Bachelor of Science degree from Temple University and received her registered nurse's training from Temple University Hospital School of Nursing. She was a nursing educator at Temple University and Mount Zion Hospital. In 1983, she earned a master's degree in public administration from the University of Southern California.

Anne Rudin

Mayor, City of Sacramento
(1983-1992)

Anne Rudin

["Sacramento in Today's Changing World," keynote address given at
United Nations Association Dinner, Sacramento, CA, November, 1990.]

*T*onight I am pleased to join with you in celebrating the 45th anniversary of the founding of the United Nations and to share with you my view of today's changing world. Among the major changes have been the values and tempo of our lives. We are living fast-moving lives with little time for introspection, family cohesion, and reinforcement of family values. We interact more with cultures and values different from our own. A new socio-cultural "underclass" has emerged, with multi-generational poverty, illiteracy, and ill health, and with little hope for improvement. This is unlike our past expectations that our future would be better than our past, that our children's lives would be better than our childhood.

But as important as all that is, it is not my subject tonight. I shall focus instead on the recent geopolitical, economic, and social changes that I see as most pertinent to U.S. cities and which require cities to have a "foreign policy." I shall identify some of the social costs of war readiness and war fighting, and will also tell you what I think has not changed.

From this we should be able to identify what we need from each other in order to create an enlightened municipal foreign policy to ensure a secure and peaceful world.

"PEOPLE POWER" has erupted on every continent (except North America, where it occurred two centuries ago and now the struggle is to hold onto it). In the Philippines, China, Poland, Czechoslovakia, the German Democratic Republic and in Central and South America, we have seen largely non-violent rebellions by the people. They have generally accepted the likelihood of short-term hardships and uncertainty for the promise of better, freer lives.

.   .   .

In this confusing and convoluted world, creditors have become debtors and debtors have become creditors. Our defeated foes of World War II are now our creditors; we, the strongest victors of World War II, are now the largest debtor (and the largest debtor to the U.N., the organization we conceived and promoted, to which we owe $522 million of the $640 million of all regular budget dues owed). In 45 years of the Cold War, the U.S. has moved from owning and underwriting Europe and Asia to being owned and underwritten by them. Both of the superpowers have been nearly bankrupted by massive borrowing, colonialism, and denial and concealment of their debts. While the U.S. president was telling his people they could spend their way out of debt, society leaders were telling their people the next five-year plan would do it. The only difference between the U.S. and U.S.S.R. economic disasters is the richer economic base from which the U.S. started its descent.

. . .

The economy mimics nature. Fluorocarbons emitted in a temperate zone produce ultraviolet leaks in polar regions; trees in the Southern Hemisphere gobble up excess CO_2 produced in the Northern Hemisphere. Wendell Wilkie's "One World" is here in economics and ecology, though not recognized yet in politics and society.

. . .

This nation has had a long history of expecting local interests to lobby to influence government domestic policy. This has often been tied to the nation's military policy. Sacramento was so involved from its very beginning. In 1862, the Big Four sold Theodore Judah's dream of a transcontinental railroad to President Lincoln. At the time, our nation was deeply troubled, engaged in a not-so-civil Civil War. Lincoln had to control the human and the natural resources of the anti-slave western territories in the war against the Confederacy, so the Big Four succeeded in winning the president's support for an initial survey and a $700,000 subsidy.

Then came the Pacific Railroad Act, which gave away free to the Central Pacific and the Union Pacific a four-hundred-foot-wide right-of-way over the entire route to the terminus in Sacramento. This required the appropriation of government, Indian, and private lands. It elicited understandable opposition, but there was a war to be won, more anti-slave states to be added. It passed.

In the 1920s, the Sacramento Chamber of Commerce, working with local government, began to lobby for federal funds. This paid off in 1933 when New Deal agencies made loans and grants for public buildings, schools, roads, parks, and other civic improvements.

. . .

Sacramento thrived during World War II!

The city continued to grow in our victorious nation. We joined the national effort to rehabilitate and rebuild Europe and Asia.

In the post-World War II era, with the U.S. engaged in a Cold War, the Korean War, and a race to the moon, federal investment in military and aerospace soared. Sacramento's private sector and local government were successful in bringing to Sacramento a significant share of those investments. Population again doubled, leading to increased demands for housing, health care, schools, recreation facilities, and shopping centers, which, in turn, produced more private sector jobs.

For the first time, county population exceeded city population. To handle the increased population and activity, and the greater distances from work and play, freeways were built, generating *more* usage which, in turn, generated the need for *more* freeways and highways.

Many state and city functions were shifted to the county government. Downtown declined as the suburbs became more attractive as places to live, work, and shop. Government in Washington and Sacramento got stronger, bigger, and more powerful. Local lobbying of Washington became even more important. The city sought its portion of revenue sharing and various other programs to build inner-cities, like the urban renewal programs of the 1950s and 60s, and historic preservation in the 70s.

Nowadays, we lobby for flood control, power and energy development, air and water quality programs, housing and redevelopment, and even cable TV.

But fighting a war, even a cold war, shifts priorities away from such local needs as roads, bridges, public buildings, air and water purity, waste disposal and sewage treatment, and energy conservation and alternatives. Local government must compete for capital against the rising national and private sector debts.

With domestic needs so tied to foreign policies that can lead to war, it is imperative that cities assert themselves on foreign and military policy, just as they do on domestic policy.

. . .

Immanuel Kant, the great 18th century philosopher, spent most of his life in Frederick the Great's Prussia, one of the most militaristic nations in history.... In his later years he denounced rulers who siphoned off all available funds to pay for their wars and called war the "depravity of human nature...without disguise." He described relations between states as "lawless." At age 70, in 1795, he acknowledged that war motivated people to innovate and exert themselves as peace did not, but warned that, unless nations reversed course, wars would grow increasingly violent, leading ultimately to a war of mutual extermination. It would leave only the peace of "the vast graveyard of the human race."

. . .

A half century later the great warrior, and still venerated military strategist, Carl Von Clausewitz, said no nation would ever carry its military action to the point of risking self-extermination.

He may be right, but can we take that chance, especially if there may be a better alternative?

We are now at the point of having to make that decision. We have the capacity for mutual nuclear annihilation, or, at least, total destruction of cities anywhere on earth, as Kant predicted. The exhausted superpowers can no longer restrain nations with less to lose (except lives) and with access to nuclear and biochemical weapons. Thus, the danger of accidental or terrorist genocidal destruction is greater than ever before. That is why cities, especially cities governed by freely elected representatives and governing in freely elected states, must now represent the ethical standards of their citizens, who have so much to lose if the values that can generate and maintain peace are not brought to bear on domestic and foreign federal policy.

There is no longer time to philosophize about ethics. It is now time to apply ethical principles to political governance. Cities like Sacramento can focus on that.

If the dangers are greater than ever before, so are the opportunities. The same super-power exhaustion and bankruptcy which has dangerously freed smaller countries and terrorists has also freed the United Nations. For the first time in its history, the U.N. can be what it was intended to be. East-West paranoia, which for so long paralyzed the Security Council, has given way to negotiation on tactics and beginning adherence to principles. The U.S.S.R. seems to seek the moderating influence of the U.N. in international conflicts and agrees with Security Council decisions without having to oppose the U.S. by exercising the old vetoes. Instead, it now says it will send military forces into the Middle East only if they are under U.N. military staff command.

.   .   .

In January of 1991, the U.S. is scheduled to begin a conference of the signers of the Limited Test Ban Treaty to try to achieve a Comprehensive Test Ban Treaty. This is supported by a number of U.S. cities and the U.S. Conference of Mayors, but the U.S. government still threatens to veto such a conclusion. If the Comprehensive Test Ban proposal is vetoed, after approval by all other signatories, controls on nuclear proliferation would be sorely weakened and would be a U.S. responsibility. If the ban on testing were extended, it would likely strengthen the Non-Proliferation Treaty and put pressure on nations which have not yet signed to sign, or on those which have not kept their pledge, to comply.

If you agree with me, please let your City Council representative and me know that you would like us to pass a resolution indicating Sacramento's support for a Comprehensive Test Ban.

This is a major time of testing for the U.N. If it can help to defuse Persian Gulf tensions and the Arab-Israeli conflict and get a Comprehensive Test Ban and a better-enforced Non-Proliferation Treaty, can it go on to help with other regional threats? Can it act to reduce the threat of terrorism and nuclear terrorism? Can it be even more effective than it has been in preventing starvation, disease, and mortality in Africa? Can it establish the experience and the institutions for reducing belligerence in a variety of hot spots which are the legacy of past colonialism and power-bloc deals? Can it address global environmental problems?

If so, the climate of each could provide unprecedented opportunities for cities like Sacramento to catch up with pressing local needs. That is why Sacramento is justified in taking a position on foreign policy.

. . .

Sacramento's opportunities to implement a peace-promoting foreign policy are great if we act in an informed way. But if the opportunities are great, so are the costs of transition from war or war-readiness booms to peace booms. We have been living in a war economy for so long, we have forgotten how a peace-promoting economy works. We are now reconciled to spending over half of the money we raise to pay past debt, and to take personal hits in entitlement and human services to reduce the deficit.

. . .

That can only mean a reduction in miliary bases, military production facilities, and the personnel required by each.

It is not surprising that persons, especially employees affected by such decisions, will challenge these reductions out of personal interest and fear for their jobs. It is perfectly appropriate for them to do so, and to ask for our help in protecting their futures. Those who will feel personally assaulted by the downside of the DOD's [Department of Defense's] decisions are unable to see them in long-range perspective and admit the "upside." The fact that the decision was anticipated makes it no less painful.

But when they petition their city officials to keep bases open, aren't they asking us to have a military and foreign policy, even though the city has no authority over military bases, and even though the base primarily exists not to benefit the employees and the city but to meet national defense needs?

A transition must occur. The secretary of Defense, under a mandate to do his share to reduce the federal budget deficit, has stated that very clearly. We need clear national goals of transition. Instead of resisting this change, Congress should be enacting legislation that will assure transitional income support and assistance to local communities to provide support for the affected individuals, their families, and the community.

It isn't enough to plan for the re-use of property, equipment and facilities that are no longer needed by the military. We must also assist the civilian employees who will no longer have jobs. Base conversions will have a dramatic impact on their careers and lives.

A model for addressing this concern exists locally. The Human Resources Committee of the Sacramento Area Commission on Mather Conversion has formed an Employment Coalition to address job loss and job creation and to help displaced workers get back into the Sacramento civilian work force.

I believe that it is just as appropriate for *you*, from an entirely different perspective, to petition the City Council to oppose or support federal actions or proposals on foreign affairs and military matters as it was for McClellan employees to do that. You, too, should be able to tell us the impact on you, your family, and our community. Indeed, you are perhaps *obliged* to do that, as well as to suggest how we might mitigate those impacts and take advantage of the new opportunities.

On another front, I would like to expand our Sister City relationships, with more attention to the exchange of trade and ideas. Both sides could benefit from a reciprocal exchange of products and services. If the Soviet Union or China has a marketing and distribution problem during this time of *their* transition to a non-military, decentralized governance, why don't we arrange to get our goods, services, and know-how into Kishinev's and Jinan's markets, offices, and universities? Why not exchange ideas with them about cleaning air and water, protecting forests, farmlands and wetlands? Why not compare experiences with housing and feeding our respective people? All this while sharing locally produced art, music, literature and theater.

.   .   .

Sacramento, for many years involved in Pacific Rim negotiations for commerce and trade, is now looking to post-1992 Europe for new business partners. No doubt, many will not want to see more foreign investment in California or Sacramento. Can we shed our ethnocentrism and egocentrism? As we become better acquainted with our counterparts in other nations, as I have with mayors throughout the world, I am more impressed with how much we have in common than with how different we are. As we meet on each other's turf, fear and distrust of unknown places and persons is diminished. And because it is easier to *espouse* the golden rule than to practice it, the residual fear and distrust still prompts a fight or flight response in the face of real or imagined threats.

I believe Sacramento *can* make it in this changing world. Indeed, we can make it quite well. We need only deal openly and respectfully with each other, being clear about what we have, what we need, and what we want. We can be creative, empathetic, and realistic as we face our changing world together.

With that combination, we can thrive on the opportunities of this dramatically changing world.

They are as full of promise as the opportunity presented upon the signing of the United Nations Charter in San Francisco 45 years ago. At that event, President Harry S Truman said, "If we had had this charter a few years ago, and above all the will to use it, millions now dead would be alive. If we should falter in our will to use it, millions now living will surely die".

Let us not falter.

Index of Issues

DORIS EARNSHAW received her Ph.D. in comparative literature at the University of California, Berkeley, in 1981. As a graduate student in the 1970s, she organized the research and translation of women poets from many languages. That effort resulted in a pioneering anthology, *The Other Voice: Twentieth Century Women Poets in Translation* (W.W. Norton, 1976). She taught in the Great Books of Western Civilization program at the University of California, Davis, where she initiated and taught a course on the stories, novels and poetry of women writers worldwide until she retired in 1993.

Type styles used: Dutch 801 Roman
Commercial Script-wp
Fonts found in WordPerfect 6.0
Paper used: James River 60lb White Recycled Offset

 PRINTED ON
RECYCLED PAPER